"In my personal experience the two h
instrumental in the successful kickof
been a part of at TreviPay. It has allo\
part of a cross functional team, where all stakeholders are in a focused
physical and mental space which allows us to democratize the design
thinking process to solve our users' needs."

*- Alesandro Meléndez, User Experience Designer, TreviPay*

"I've been able to apply this technique a few times now. Thanks to you,
I now have a process that I can use every time I need to do product discovery when there are time and availability constraints from the product
stakeholders."

*- Ruben Betancourt, Head of Product, Tango.io*

"Reviewing the two hour design sprint resources with the team set
everyone up with the right expectations. Given the common foundation,
we were able to parse which aspects to cover during the two hour design
sprint (reviewing opportunities + user personas, exploring the problem +
goals / needs, and ideating solutions that will address the pains / motivations through low fidelity sketches) and afterwards (building prototype
solutions and testing with customers). This model enabled us to better include remote team members and experiment + learn even more quickly."

*- Diana Stepner, Head of Product, Chan Zuckerberg Initiative*

"The process creates space to surface problems, acknowledges technological constraints, and aligns your team. In my experience, even the people
who claim to be the least creative provide some of the best solutions. As
the team unpacks the intended problem, it naturally surfaces additional
and even adjacent problems that would have a greater impact on their
business. This discovery often comes with more refined, cost-effective
solutions that don't require as much time or resources to deliver. What a
win for your team! More evidence that this process works."

*- Brian Cox, Founder and CEO, Digital Bullpen*

# SOLVING PROBLEMS IN 2 HOURS

## How to Brainstorm and Create Solutions with Two Hour Design Sprints

### TERESA CAIN

**Solving Problems in 2 Hours How to Brainstorm and Create Solutions with Two Hour Design Sprints (2023)**

**Copyright @ 2023 by Teresa Cain**

ISBN: 979-8-9876868-0-5

Published by Lucid Creative Press

Requests to publish work from this book should be sent to: hello@lucidcreativepress.com

Foreword: Bill Staikos

Interlude: John Kille

Cover and Interior Design: Kerry Ellis

Editor: Melissa Kearney

https://www.lucidcreativepress.com

*To my product and user experience community that has supported me on my journey by attending conferences, workshops, on-demand training, podcasts and online events. To my husband, kids, parents, friends, colleagues at TreviPay, fellow alumni and professors at Rockhurst University's Executive MBA program, and fellow students and professors at Carnegie Mellon University's Master of Integrated Innovation for Products and Services. Thank you all for helping make this book a reality!*

# Contents

# FOREWORD BY BILL STAIKOS

Design thinking is a problem-solving approach that has been widely adopted by organizations, designers, and innovators around the world. It is a human-centered approach that emphasizes empathy, experimentation, and iteration as key elements in the design process. Design thinking has its roots in the design community, but it has been adapted and adopted by many different fields, including business, technology, education, and healthcare.

Design sprints are a specific application of design thinking that originated in the technology industry. Design sprints are typically short, focused, and intensive problem-solving events that are designed to produce rapid prototyping and testing of new ideas and products. The goal of a design sprint is to move quickly from idea to prototype and then to validation, with the aim of reducing the time and risk associated with traditional product development cycles. Some design sprints last for a full week, while others may spread out over a period of several weeks. Regardless of the format, design sprints follow a structured process that includes problem definition, ideation, prototyping, testing, and iteration.

The popularity of a design sprint can be attributed to its ability to bring teams together to focus on a specific problem and quickly produce tangible outcomes. Design sprints are seen as a way to overcome traditional roadblocks in the design process, such as lengthy approval processes, lack of collaboration, and resistance to change. The evolution of design thinking into design sprints represents a shift toward a more agile and efficient approach to problem-solving and innovation. By incorporating design thinking principles and applying them to the rapid prototyping of new ideas, design sprints offer a new way to bring together diverse perspectives and quickly test and validate new solutions.

The consistent pressure to develop new products and services, solve customer and business problems quickly, and meet the ever-evolving needs of consumers are just some of the reasons why design sprints have become critical business tools. The pandemic only seems to have exacerbated this, where a company's need to remain competitive and relevant often means turning ideas into tangible outcomes in the shortest time possible.

## The Importance of Design Sprints

My professional background includes leading Customer Experience teams at some of the biggest brands in financial services. My teams used design sprints as a framework to help our business partners and stakeholders achieve their goals by providing a structured approach to problem-solving, and, in some cases, product development. They allowed our teams to rapidly prototype and test ideas, reducing the risk associated with launching a new product or service. By prototyping and testing early, teams could identify potential roadblocks and make course corrections before it was too late. This led to more efficient use of resources and ultimately accelerated our return on investment.

Design sprints also fostered collaboration and encouraged cross-functional teams to work together. By bringing together a diverse group of stakeholders through the design sprint process, we ensured that everyone was aligned on the problem for which we were solving and the solution being proposed. This led to faster, better decision-making, it created an environment for greater innovation, and a working environment defined by efficacy.

When our teams were leading design sprints, we delivered a structured approach to problem-solving. The five day process we consistently followed provided a clear roadmap for teams to follow, and the structured activities ensured that all aspects of the problems we were focused on were thoroughly explored. This led our organization to deliver more informed decisions, and a greater understanding of the challenges and opportunities associated with a particular project. If the solution meant a less optimal outcome for the business, but right for the customer or employee, at least we approached the final solution *"eyes wide open."*

Finally, because design sprints are flexible and adaptable tools, the teams I have led and been part of have been able to apply the design sprint framework to a wide range of problems and projects. The toolkit also allowed us to customize it to suit the specific needs of any organization given its flexibility. This meant that design sprints would be used to solve complex problems across a variety of functions – from technology and product, to operations and finance.

## Design Sprints in Action

Imagine a team of mortgage professionals in a large industry that was tasked with finding ways to better serve the needs of underserved borrowers. This was the team I was part of in early 2020. After conducting market research and speaking with potential homeowners, the team realized that these future home buyers were in need of a more streamlined and efficient way to manage savings for their home and improve their finances. The research also showed the importance of specific partners in the process.

To address this problem faced by thousands of potential homeowners around the country, the team decided to use a design sprint to create a new product that would help these underserved borrowers better manage their finances through an app-based solution. Over the course of five days, the team worked through a series of structured activities, including brainstorming sessions, prototyping, and user testing.

At the end of the design sprint, the team had created a working prototype of a financial management tool specifically designed for the personas for whom they were building a solution. The tool allowed these borrowers to easily track progress against savings, monitor their credit score, and generate reports they could use with third-party providers like mortgage counselors. In addition, their counselors also would be able to see their progress whereby they could prepare more effectively for meetings with their clients. The team presented the prototype to a group of potential homeowners, who provided valuable feedback and suggestions for improvement. With this feedback in hand, the team was able to refine and improve the product before launching it more broadly. It was the first time the company employed this methodology.

The design sprint was a success, and the new financial management and savings app quickly became popular among underserved borrowers. The tool not only helped them better manage their finances, but it also helped counselors better serve this important customer segment, leading to increased customer satisfaction and loyalty.

## Benefits We Can Achieve Through Design Sprints

Perhaps the most significant benefit of a design sprint in my experience is the ability to rapidly prototype and test ideas, reducing the risk associated with launching a new product or service that doesn't meet the needs of your customer. This leads to more efficient use of resources and lower technical debt when delivering new digital capabilities. Another important benefit of design sprints is the ability to foster collaboration, and encourage cross-functional teams to work together. By bringing together a diverse group of stakeholders, the design sprint process ensures alignment across functions. Through collaboration, productivity is positively impacted as teams are able to achieve more output in a shorter period of time.

In addition to the benefits mentioned above, design sprints also deliver a very specific practical advantage. Specifically, because traditional design sprints comprised five days of work, it allowed teams to compress months of work into just five days, which saves time and resources.

When we consider the mortgage industry example mentioned earlier, we were able to model the reduction in technical debt based on similar innovations and how they were delivered. And because we were able to bring a product to market more quickly, we also were able to quantify the increased revenue impact gained by employing a five day sprint.

## Compressing Design Sprint to 2 Hours from 5 Days

Throughout my career, my teams and I have flexed the design

thinking methodology, and design sprint toolkit, to fit the needs of the business. Teresa Cain is a business leader who I admire and respect, and she has taken a concept that reshaped how companies approach problem solving, and she shows how teams and leaders can further compress the design sprint to solve for specific types of business needs. Not only does this book provide a framework for delivering on a two hour sprint, it further pushes the envelope of existing business thinking.

I applaud Teresa's courage to challenge the status quo and create a new framework to expedite a decision-making process that adapts well to the demands of rapidly releasing new features to customers. I can say there were definitely scenarios where our Business Transformation teams could have used her methodology in a past life. To note, at the large mortgage industry player mentioned earlier, my team trained all of our agile teams in design thinking, and building design sprints into their day-to-day work. If they had employed Teresa's methodology to specific backlog items or within specific ceremonies, they would have further improved their efficacy, and achieved their OKRs *(Objectives & Key Results)* more quickly.

So whether you're a small start-up or a large corporation, two hour design sprints can help you turn your ideas into tangible outcomes in the shortest time possible. If you're looking to improve specific areas of your business, or simply want to explore new ways of solving business and customer problems, consider incorporating two hour design sprints into your work. The benefits are many and varied, and the results speak for themselves. Teresa Cain's new book will get you there, and more quickly!

# *PREFACE*

We've all been there at one point or another – sitting in a room with colleagues from across the organization spitballing ideas, problems and solutions about how to grow the business. This scenario was commonplace before COVID-19 disrupted the workplace and workflow as we knew it. Even before the pandemic, I typically prepared and organized multiple design sprints for my team. I couldn't have predicted in a million years how a chain of events outside of my control would compel businesses, families and society to adapt to survive.

It was the fall of 2019. On the one hand, I knew my personal life would be changing soon. As a mother of two working full-time for more than 15 years in high-stress, high-reward technology organizations and navigating work-life balance as a female leader in tech, I thought I was prepared for anything. However, work-life balance was about to get trickier. I was expecting my third child and the clock was ticking, giving me just a few months before my due date. I was working remotely that week, a rare occurrence for me. In hindsight, it was an ironic foreshadowing clue of what was to come with COVID-19. I had been working with an international client on a difficult project launch that was very demanding of my time and patience. Navigating work-life balance was made a bit more complicated due to the time zone change; I needed to be available to join 4 a.m. calls regularly. That same week, a colleague asked me to join a critical multi-day design sprint for a new feature we were evaluating as a team. So, I pivoted and went into the office for the three day design sprint. The sprint was troubleshooting a new product feature managing customer hierarchy within a workflow process. On the first day of the design sprint, I sat in a room with more than 20 other team leaders from across the organization, including account management, product management, engineering, support, underwriting and sales. We started out by exploring why each of us was participating. I joined the session in a focused mindset to ignore distractions. I left my laptop at my desk. I was well-equipped with snacks, water and my phone set to vibrate, only for emergencies. About two hours into the session, we were in the middle of an intensive brainstorming session with sticky notes scattering our ideas all across the whiteboard at the front of the room. At that point, I needed to step out of the room. My abrupt departure was not for reasons you might imagine; I did not go into labor in the middle of the meeting. Instead, I had received a phone call that I let go to voicemail, followed by a text and another phone call. This was obviously urgent and was coming directly from a key client. I promptly texted the client back and as subtle as a woman in her third trimester is able to achieve, I excused myself from the room. After a few minutes of discussion with the client, it was clear I would need to step out of the session for much longer than anticipated. I pulled aside the design sprint moderator, a highly esteemed colleague and visionary, and let him know I would have to step out and join later. I proceeded to jump onto an urgent phone call with the client, engineering, and product teams to discuss an issue. Although I was able to join the design sprint again, I had missed out on key questions and decisions the group had answered about building a complex system of hierarchies for clients. For me, it exposed one of the drawbacks of multi-day design sprints. My experience with multi-day design sprints is one shared by other stakeholders. Design sprints are important and solve critical business problems. However, carving out two, three, four, or five full workdays to focus on problems within an organization means other critical needs are ignored during that time. COVID-19 disrupted the workplace in ways big and small, requiring organizations to become nimble and flexible, including the adoption of the two hour design sprint concept. However, even before the coronavirus pandemic reached our shores, it was clear to me that many organizations were already reducing five day design sprints to a few days, one half of a workday or less, including ours.

At TreviPay, a leader in global payments and invoicing, we had already shortened design sprints to a few days. Although we had many successful in-person, multi-day design sprints under our belts, that concept changed with COVID-19 when operations went 100% remote for our product and technology organization. I recall the first design sprint I led after the pandemic hit the United States. It was March 2020. I had just recently returned from maternity leave, and I managed to go into the office for an entire day before lockdowns began. It was an odd day to go to work. Conversations among colleagues percolated about the severity of the disease and how it was spread. The morning started with coffee side chats and high fives. By noon, the vibe took a dramatic turn with communication from the executive team to work remotely the rest of the day, per county public health guidelines.

I remember thinking that COVID-19 would likely be a short-lived experience, after all I had lived through the 2009 swine flu pandemic[1], 2014 Ebola outbreak[2] and 2016 Zika outbreak.[3] However, weeks passed with the return to the office nowhere on the horizon. In fact, our organization had no plans to return until the Summer or Fall of 2022. We extended remote work due to COVID-19 and because we were moving to a new building for more space and better collaboration options. In the meantime, I had a critical business problem to solve that involved scoring customers that were not paying their bills. This was an issue that had been on my radar for quite some time. Originally, I had plans to utilize a third-party vendor; instead, we decided to build our own solution internally. April rolled around, and I decided to run a virtual design sprint to get moving on the concept. I began to research how other organizations were conducting virtual design sprints. To my surprise and dismay, I found nothing at all. So, I created a process and jammed with my team on a frontier concept, a process that would help shape the landscape for all design sprints going forward at TreviPay, a hybrid work organization. We were already condensing the timeframe of design sprints to one, two or three days, so why not a couple hours? My first execution of the condensed design sprint was four hours, then three, and onto success with two hour design sprints. After conducting more than 20 two hour design sprints with our product and UX teams at TreviPay in both 2021 and 2022, I pitched the concept modification at several user conferences to share the successes for our organization. I was delighted to discover from session attendees that other organizations experienced challenges with multi-day design sprint methods and had already made modifications of their own or were looking for tips on how to execute a shorter design sprint without sacrificing the end goal. This inspired me to lead workshops, conduct on-demand training and further informed my decision to write this book to help other technology organizations learn best practices and drive success with condensed and effective two hour design sprints. *Solving Problems in 2 Hours: How to Brainstorm and Create Solutions with Two Hour Design*

*Sprints* examines advantages of a two hour design sprint process, provides concrete examples to be effective, and gives readers an insider's look from technology leaders who have executed two hour design sprints after they participated in a conference session, training or live workshop session.

# *INTRODUCTION*

B efore we dive right into how to conduct two hour design sprints, let's explore why you should consider implementing two hour design sprints at your organization. The exponential growth of self-service technology apps, websites and products have created the demand to deliver features faster to customers while in a remote or hybrid working environment. There is an opportunity to help organizations learn how to solve problems faster and accelerate solutions using two hour design sprints. In the United States alone, more than 627,000 businesses launch each year, and over 595,000 close.[1] I want to help start-ups and long-established businesses to survive and thrive. Design sprints are an investment that technology organizations – large and small – should be investing in to solve business problems and to help accelerate the growth of their product roadmap. Businesses that are not continuously looking for new and efficient ways to solve problems risk falling behind competitors or worse, getting swallowed up by them. During my Executive Master of Business Administration program at Rockhurst University, a degree I pursued before starting a second Master's in Integrated Innovation for Products and Services from Carnegie Mellon University, I examined why businesses fail, focusing on strategy and innovation for businesses and professionals. We studied an analysis published in 2003 in the Harvard Business Review, a transformative time for high tech companies. It examined how Apple in 2001 introduced the iTunes store and the iPod, revolutionizing portable devices and transforming the consumer experience for digital media and entertainment. For me, the biggest takeaway from, *"The Quest for Resilience*[2]*"* that appeared in the September 2003 of Harvard Business Review is the following quote that's seared into my memory: *"In a turbulent age, the only dependable advantage is a superior capacity for reinventing your business model before circumstances force you to."* Strategic renewal is important for every organization. Although this piece was published two decades ago, its relevance is as important today as ever. COVID-19 forced organizations to adapt or wither on the vine. Resilient organizations seek opportunities to grow their teams and grow market share, foster a collaborative culture and solve problems with and for their customers before it's too late. Every day is a new opportunity for start-ups and established businesses to automate products and solutions or identify and solve problems for internal and external customers. We must always continue to innovate and improve efficiency. That's exactly what two hour design sprints are designed to achieve. The best way to do that is to talk to your customers.

## Tactical Value You Will Get Out of This Book:

- How to solve problems in two hours using the concept of two hour design sprints;

- The difference between design thinking and design sprint methods;

- The value of using two hour design sprints, and the advantages over five day design sprint or design thinking methods;

- The prep work involved in running two hour design sprints;

- How to conduct virtual and in-person two hour design sprints;

- How to train teams to run two hour design sprints;

- How to use collaborative online tools to run two hour design sprints;

- How to save your organization thousands of dollars; and,

- How to help your organization release product features faster to clients.

# PART I:
# UNDERSTAND
# THE VALUE OF
# TWO HOUR
# DESIGN SPRINTS

**CHAPTER 1**

# *WHAT ARE TWO HOUR DESIGN SPRINTS?*

*Solving Problems in 2 Hours: How to Brainstorm and Create Solutions with Two Hour Design Sprints* gives you the tools you need to create more opportunities for success as an organization by increasing the frequency of problem-solving and accelerating the delivery of solutions for your customers. In this chapter, we will talk about the success of an adaptation to a two hour design sprint process using a hybrid methodology created from design thinking and design sprint methods.

## Inspired by Design Thinking and Design Sprint Methods

Two hour design sprints are inspired by the design thinking

and design sprint methods and are best used for accelerating concepts with problem-solving. If you're not familiar with the difference between design thinking and design sprints, a design sprint is derived from the design thinking method *(see Figure 1.1)*. Design thinking methods might take several months that can stretch into years to really develop and think through a problem. With design thinking methods, you could spend six to 12 months empathizing, defining, ideating, prototyping and testing your problem. As for a timeline, no time constraints existed on the original construct for design thinking, much like the waterfall SDLC *(software development life cycle)* methodology in which you shipped a product when it was done. In other words, there was no deadline to meet or beat. Most organizations do not have the luxury to spend months and years researching a problem before delivering a solution. Behold, the genesis of the design sprint was born.

# Design Thinking[1] vs. Design Sprints[2]

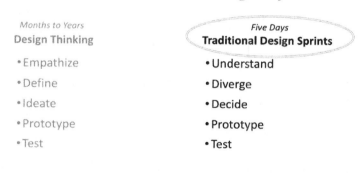

| *Months to Years*<br>Design Thinking | *Five Days*<br>**Traditional Design Sprints** |
| --- | --- |
| • Empathize | • Understand |
| • Define | • Diverge |
| • Ideate | • Decide |
| • Prototype | • Prototype |
| • Test | • Test |

*Figure 1.1*

Many companies learned that five day design sprints were most successful for solving big problems with very large budgets. Most organizations don't have the company resources like Google to conduct five day design sprints with regularity or have the budget to pay third party consulting firms that cost anywhere from $10,000 to $200,000. Five day design sprints pose substantive challenges for start-ups with limited resources, team members, and budgets. That's why self-led two hour design sprints present a perfect fit for small, midsize and large organizations to meet their goals and achieve success.

## Creator of the Design Sprint Process Jake Knapp and Google Ventures

Much like Don Norman is referred to as the godfather of UX, which we'll cover more in Chapter 4: *"History of UX,"* Jake Knapp and the team at Google Ventures *(GV)* invented the term design sprints that are derived from the concept of design thinking. Knapp and the team at GV improved a process that previously took years to complete. Through trial and error, they simplified and streamlined the design thinking concept that organizations could use to solve problems in five days. In their iteration of the five day design sprint, which I'll refer to as a traditional design sprint, they created five stages with variations. The stages of a five day design sprint are: understand, diverge, decide, prototype, and test. Jake Knapp and the team at GV released the book *Sprint: Solve Big Problems And Test New Ideas In Just Five Days (Sprint)* in 2016.[3] Their concept gained fast adoption in the technology sector across some of the world's leading technology companies.

## Remote Five Day Design Sprints by Jake Knapp, John Zeratsky and Jackie Colburn

Just as the COVID-19 pandemic forced TreviPay and other organizations to look for modified ways to conduct virtual design sprints, the creators of *Sprint* also made modifications to their process. In 2023, they added a guide to conduct a remote five day design sprint and templates available in Miro,[4] Mural[5] and Invision[6] that look pretty slick for solving large problems. While I have not yet tested this new template for conducting a five day design sprint, I look forward to trying it out to see how it compares to my two hour virtual format. After all, they blazed the trail to marry design thinking with design sprints and both inspired me to pursue two hour design sprints. To check out their guide, visit the Design Sprint website.[7]

Take note what Jake Knapp, John Zeratsky and Jackie Colburn, the creators of the newly modified remote five day design sprint said about remote design sprints: ***"When we published Sprint in 2016, we recommended running Design Sprints in person."***[8] In their book *Sprint,*[9] they referenced how technology for remote sprints wasn't ready yet. While they don't mention the COVID-19 pandemic specifically, virtual tool adoption was fast-tracked during the lockdowns that precipitated the adoption of remote workforces at organizations around the world. While still using a five day model for the remote design sprint, it is interesting to see the agenda and additional tools they recommend including Zoom[10] for video conferencing, Miro[11] for a virtual whiteboard, Basecamp[12] for team discussion, Userinterviews.com[13] for recruiting customers and GoToMeeting[14] for interviewing customers.

In addition to their recommended tools, Knapp, Zertasky and Colburn reference AJ&Smart's[15] pick of tools including Whereby[16] for interviewing customers. We will talk more about AJ&Smart in Chapter 2: ***"Solve Any Problem"*** and dive into third-party consulting firms that run design sprints. Keep in mind that AJ&Smart is particularly popular not only for facilitating a design sprint, but participating and contributing elite expertise in design thinking, product and business strategy, user-centric design, prototyping, and technology, according to their website.[17]

## Impact of COVID-19 Pandemic

A number of consulting firms, webinars and books currently push a five day design sprint model that hasn't adapted to changes brought on by COVID-19. That's when many organizations evolved their thinking to run a fully remote or hybrid model of design sprints. Even before the pandemic, five day or even multi-day design sprints didn't work optimally for many organizations. On the one hand, they limit the number of design sprints an organization can conduct per year because of the time and resources they soak up. On the other hand, the multi-day commitment creates a disadvantage for organizations who otherwise would benefit by conducting a number of two hour design sprints per month to solve more problems. It's time to talk about the evolution in the design sprint space to a leaner, more innovative, effective and feasible approach, whether virtual or in person.

Design sprints traditionally are conducted in person over five days, and often moderated by third-party companies. This format is outdated and busts budgets. I have found success with shorter two hour design sprints that recognize budget constraints and the flexibilities required for remote work arrangements that are the new norm for many firms in the technology space. Conducting the design sprint on your own as an organization also allows you to tailor the process for your teams. Two hour design sprints help organizations deliver value-driven features even faster by simplifying the design thinking process. Organizations no longer need to invest in third parties to run extensive and expensive five day design sprints. Internal product and UX teams can run two hour design sprints with just as much, if not more success.

## Benefits of Two Hour Design Sprints

The two hour design sprint process creates more opportunities for success by increasing the frequency and speed you can solve problems as an organization. The topline goals for conducting a two hour design sprint process are to:

- Accelerate your product roadmap and push high-value features to your clients faster and with better value;

- Create more buy-in with internal stakeholders;

- Conduct multiple design sprints in a week or month to problem-solve concepts and identify ideas and solutions faster and more efficiently;

- Use a hybrid methodology and a template that is repeatable so you can conduct multiple two hour design sprints virtually or in person on your own instead of using an expensive third-party consulting firm.

CHAPTER 2

# *SOLVE ANY PROBLEM*

It is easy to think you have all the answers to meet your customers needs and wants. However, until you are able to first understand their problems, you won't have the right solutions. Although this process will not solve problems *for* you, it will empower you to use design thinking and design sprint methodologies in a condensed format. And that will enable you to solve problems for your customers more productively, effectively and efficiently. If you consistently use this method, you can rest assured you will focus on the right problems without wasting time, money and resources that otherwise would be expended with a full five day design sprint or other UX methods.

## Startups or Small Organizations

As an entrepreneur with a decade of experience working with startups, the biggest challenge I have observed over the years is the lack of time and resources. Depending on the stage of your company, you may also have another full-time job or perhaps you have launched into success receiving multiple rounds of seed funding. Either way, in a smaller and newer organization just getting its feet wet, typically the product ideas and roadmap are being created by one or a handful of individuals. Two hour design sprints are a much more digestible task to organize and complete rather than dedicating five days to new concepts. It also fits better in the workflow of lean, agile, or Kanban methodologies to integrate newly vetted ideas in the next sprint, whether you are on week one or week four of a sprint cycle. If you don't have a development team just yet, don't fret! Two hour design sprints can help you create and vet the highest priority items from potential customers before you have developers build it. In the end, this ultimately saves time and money. If you're a startup looking for more resources to help launch your organization into the next phase, take a look at Pipeline Entrepreneurs[1] and Mass Challenge.[2] Both organizations take applications from firms across various revenue streams, including those in their infancy to those with more than $10 million in annual revenue. They are equipped to help you grow into the next stage. I had the opportunity to work with Pipeline Entrepreneurs while completing my Executive MBA at Rockhurst University. It is remarkable to consider the impact this organization has had on the community, accumulating hundreds of startup success stories over the years. Mass Challenge also has fostered notable successful ventures and has helped launch thousands of startups to productive growth and expansion.

## Roadmap Growth for Entrepreneurs

As you look to grow new features in your roadmap, it can be easy to just want to design and build. This is where strategic, targeted problem-solving comes into play. Deploying two hour design sprints will help make sure you are solving the right problems for the users for whom you are building your product. It's easy to think we have all the right answers and know exactly what our customers want. However, it's critical to take the steps to ensure you see eye to eye with your customers and get their feedback from the get-go. It's tempting to want to get your solution out the door as fast as possible. But be mindful this approach invites sloppy work that could miss the mark if the product is released before vetting out the right solutions. What's more, you could miss out on opportunities to make your solution even better. I recommend starting with a few features or ideas you could explore on your own or as a small team for your first two hour design sprint. I think you will be pleasantly surprised to discover how many ideas you're able to move from your roadmap into development more efficiently.

## Lack of Internal Stakeholders or Customers

Next, let's talk about other limitations confronting startups. Many entrepreneurs burn the midnight oil to build the next big thing and are stretched thin on time, money and resources. You may not have staff or have customers to bring into the process. If you have a small team or are even a team of one, this is a great time to recruit participants who are knowledgeable in the field. For instance, let's say you are building a consumer medical application to track the time of day to take prescription medications. You would need a few different personas to pull into the process to vet the design of the product. If you are not familiar with personas, we will get more into that later, but for now, personas are users who represent the target audience that will use or interact with your solution. For your new medical prescription app, for instance, you might have four personas: Doctor, Pharmacist, Patient and Caretaker. For your first two hour design sprint, you could look to recruit a few stakeholders in each persona. If that becomes too challenging to do on your own, you could hire a service, such as Usertesting.com[3] or

UserInterviews.com[4] to outsource this piece of the puzzle. You would pay the vendor to recruit stakeholders or users for you. I have used Usertesting.com to help secure user interviews and they are easy to work with and have very reasonable pricing. Usertesting.com is a great solution if you don't yet have any customers or are wanting to test an idea, prototype or design before you bring it to customers. This vendor will find your target customers for you and will even run the feedback sessions on your behalf.

## Large Organizations

Large organizations have a different set of challenges than startups or small organizations. Most often, the lack of internal stakeholders and customers is not the issue. Instead, the big obstacle is coordinating schedules from the right stakeholders and customers. This is where two hour design sprints hit the sweet spot compared to five day design sprints. It is much easier to bring 15-20 stakeholders from across the organization together in a room – or virtually – for two hours rather than for five days. The other notable challenge at large organizations is determining what problem to solve or when to break down complex problems into smaller ones.

### When to Use Five Day versus Two Hour Design Sprints

Five day design sprints are really fantastic and work great for tackling complex problems. Perhaps your organization is going to spin off a brand new line of business and you have the flexibility to schedule a five day design sprint with say, a three-month to six-month lead time. With the size and scope of the design sprint, it is acceptable if not every stakeholder is available to attend every moment of the full five days. On the other hand, two hour design sprints are intended for small to medium problems that don't have the leeway to be scheduled six months from now. For example, this situation calls for a design sprint to be scheduled within one to two weeks and requires participation and full engagement from all stakeholders for the two hour session. Whether your organization is large or small, two hour design sprints create more opportunities to solve more problems. It's entirely possible to run multiple two hour design sprints on a large problem and still spend less time than a traditional five day design sprint *(see figure 2.1)*.

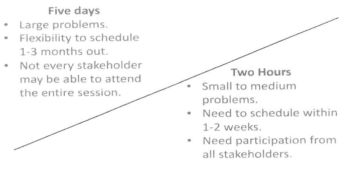

**Five days**
- Large problems.
- Flexibility to schedule 1-3 months out.
- Not every stakeholder may be able to attend the entire session.

**Two Hours**
- Small to medium problems.
- Need to schedule within 1-2 weeks.
- Need participation from all stakeholders.

*Figure 2.1*

## Choosing a Problem

Two hour design sprints are ideal for features you are looking to complete and roll out in less than six to nine months. Determining whether this is the best tool to meet your organization's needs will depend on the type of problem you are solving and how quickly you could pull together necessary stakeholders to conduct the design sprint. For engineering teams collaborating on a solution or physical product, I've implemented the highest value item from the two hour design sprint as soon as the next sprint[5] cycle. On the other hand, I've also planned and scheduled them a few quarters out depending on the priority of the features.

Problems that make the best choice for two hour design sprints include:

- Items on your backlog

- Ideas already in a discovery stage

- A client request that has a quick delivery date request

- Exploring a new industry or persona

If you have a large or complex problem and want to use two hour design sprints instead of the traditional five days, you can choose to break it down into a few two hour design sprints. For example, I have spread out design sprints to tackle complex reporting dashboards meant for different user personas and roles. If you are able to break a large problem or Epic[6] into three problem areas or user personas[7] to conduct a total of three design sprints, this bite-sized approach still would allow you to condense your problem-solving session from 15 days to a more digestible six hours.

## When to Use a Moderator or Third Party Consulting Firm

One notable benefit of a large organization is having a larger budget. I have used third-party firms to help moderate five day design sprints with price tags ranging from $10,000 to more than $100,000. Another cost-effective benefit of the two hour design sprint is you don't need to hire a moderator or third-party consulting firm to run it. However, if you prefer outside help and the budget allows, there are some great third-party firms available to run your design sprint, no matter the length including: Design Sprint SA,[8] AJ & Smart[9] and Udacity.[10] However, I strongly recommend running two hour design sprints on your own before turning to a costly third-party firm.

## School, Home or Professional Settings

Deploying two hour design sprints as a problem-solving tool is not limited to technology organizations. In fact, I've had attendees join workshops who used this accelerated problem-solving method as a group project in a classroom setting. Whereas I have not witnessed two hour design sprints used to solve arguments in the home such as whose responsibility it is to do the laundry, I have seen the methods applied in other professional settings, including interior design, architecture and construction teams to generate ideas for home building and design solutions.

## Books on Five Day Design Sprints

After reading this book and factoring in your organization's unique needs, you ultimately may decide two hour design sprints are not for you or your organization for one reason or another. So, I'd like to provide you with additional resources for five day design sprints. As mentioned in Chapter 1, *"What are Two Hour Design Sprints,"* two hour design sprints are derived from both design thinking and design sprint methodologies. Notably, Jake Knapp and the team at GV wrote a book that breaks it down in a user-friendly format: *Sprint: How to Solve Big Problems and Test New Ideas in Just Five Days.* This is a fantastic book and a great resource if you want to build a methodology that works best for your organization, whether it's a full five day design sprint or less. Some other great reads that break down five day design sprints include: *Design Sprint: A Practical Guidebook for Building Great Digital Products* by Richard Banfield and *The GV Model Guide: A guide for Google Ventures Design Sprint* by Tenny Pinheiro.

### Sprint: How to Solve Big Problems and Test New Ideas in Just Five Days by Jake Knapp, John Zeratsky & Braden Kowitz from Google Ventures[11]

Obviously, I'm a big fan of their book and the enterprising methodologies from the GV team. Their innovative design process derived from design thinking became a springboard for me to launch and modify a two hour design sprint that adapts for virtual or hybrid applications in the workplace. According to the *Sprint* book website,[12] the book is for *"anyone with a big opportunity, problem, or idea who needs to get answers today."*

We will dive more into the challenges posed by five day design sprints in Chapter 3: *"Evolution of the Design Sprint."* I can tell you one of the biggest challenges is the lack of instant gratification. Your organization won't get answers *"today"* with a five day design sprint. Instead, you might get answers after a week or more if you factor in the recommended prep time required to run a five day design sprint. With that being said, I still think five day design sprints are valuable for large, complex problems. I recommend the two hour design sprint method examined in this book for solving small- to medium-sized problems. This modified process eliminates some of the obstacles that come with the five day method, including the additional expense, navigating remote collaboration for five full days, locking in the availability of stakeholders for 40 hours, losing productive time from the team and waiting for a solution for five days, instead of reaching a consensus in two hours.

### Design Sprint: A Practical Guidebook for Building Great Digital Products by Richard Banfield[13]

According to the authors Richard Banfield, C. Todd Lombardo and Trace Wax, *"This practical guide shows you exactly what a design sprint involves and how you can incorporate the process into your organization."* While based on the five day design sprint model, I recommend this user-friendly guide for beginners to seasoned leaders to help implement design sprints at your organization.

### The GV Model Guide: A guide for Google Ventures Design Sprint by Tenny Pinheiro[14]

According to the author Tenny Pinheiro, *"this book is a must-have to any Design Sprint Master out there in the field running Design Sprints. It is full of best-practices and straight to the point information about the Google Ventures' Design Sprint methodology."* This book offers a quick read with additional insights about running design sprints that might prove useful for your organization.

## Other Two Hour Design Sprint Methods

As mentioned in the *Preface,* shorter design sprint methods – including two hour design sprints – are being practiced at other organizations besides TreviPay. I developed and evolved a method with support from my team that could be applied virtually to accommodate our remote workforce, using collaborative whiteboard tools like Figma FigJam[15]. While putting together additional research for this book, I came across blogs from product and UX field experts implementing their own version of two hour design sprint processes adapted from a five day model. I want to make sure I give credit to those who also have successfully implemented shorter two hour design sprints at their organizations. Each of their methods is unique to what worked well for them but all are a rendition of the five day design sprint process.

Much like the adaptation of agile methodologies which we will discuss more in Chapter 3: *"Evolution of the Design Sprint,"* design sprint methods are tailored to suit the needs of each organization. It's not a one-size-fits-all format. Many successful methods exist in addition to the two hour design sprint process outlined in this book, including those implemented by organizations and thought leaders found in the following section. You will notice each of the agendas created by these thought leaders is adapted from the five day process, but customized to accommodate an approach that works best for their respective organizations. One consistent theme across all approaches, including the one in the book, is including the how might we *(HMW)* exercise which we will discuss more on in Chapter 7 ***"Stage 2 Explore the Problem."***

*2-hour Sprint for Busy Stakeholders* by Justine Win[16] features a 123 minute session including setting a long-term goal, making a map, asking the experts, the HMW exercise, solution sketching and sticky decision.

*The 2 hour Design Sprint* by Chis Illuk[17] features 122 minutes including the HMW exercise, affinity mapping, presenting insights from user interviews, customer journey mapping, success metrics, crazy 8's[18] and solution sketching.

*Lessons Learnt from a 2-hour Design Sprint* by Ruben Cardoso[19] dedicates 60-120 minutes to user journey mapping, the HMW exercise, crazy 8s, dot voting, paper prototyping and testing prototypes.

*2 Hour Design Sprint UX Strat Workshop* by Brooke Katalinich[20] includes problem framing and problem statement, affinity mapping, presenting and voting on themes, Fast 4's, a rendition on crazy 8's, voting on designs and final sharing.

*Designing an onboarding experience in a 2-hour design sprint* by Martin Ganon[21] includes the HMW exercise, lightning demos, storyboarding, a four step sketch, prototyping and usability testing.

If you gain just one take-away from this book, I hope one of the tools presented here in our hybrid methodology speaks to you to help create what success looks like for your organization. I hope you are also able to understand how the process can be modified to fit the needs of your organization. Before you know it, you will be conducting two hour design sprints and solving more problems with more efficiency to help grow your business.

**CHAPTER 3**

# *EVOLUTION*
# *OF THE*
# *DESIGN SPRINT*

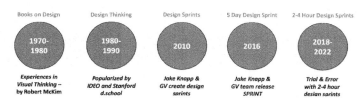

| Books on Design | Design Thinking | Design Sprints | 5 Day Design Sprint | 2-4 Hour Design Sprints |
|---|---|---|---|---|
| 1970-1980 | 1980-1990 | 2010 | 2016 | 2018-2022 |
| Experiences in Visual Thinking – by Robert McKim | Popularized by IDEO and Stanford d.school | Jake Knapp & GV create design sprints | Jake Knapp & GV team release SPRINT | Trial & Error with 2-4 hour design sprints |

*Figure 3.1*

The concept of design thinking and design sprints have evolved over time dating back to the 1970s and 1980s *(see Figure 3.1)*. One book in particular, *Experiences in Visual Thinking* by Robert McKim,[1] is attributed for the uptick in user experience methods. Design thinking was later popularized by IDEO[2] and Stanford d.school[3] in the late 1980s and 1990s. A few decades later, Jake Knapp and the team at GV started to conduct what was later called design sprints on concepts within the organization. In Chapter 1, we took a look at *Sprint: Solve Big Problems And Test New Ideas In Just Five Days*[4] published by Jake Knapp and the team at GV in 2016. Fast forward to 2018, and a lot of trial and error was underway. Five day design sprints gobbled up time and staffing resources. Organizations started reducing those commitments to four days, three days, two days, and eventually compressed the sprints all the way down to what's being practiced today: two hour design sprints. Two hour and four hour design sprints were discovered through trial and error based on what worked well at several of the organizations I worked for, and with, including product and UX communities and beyond. In addition, the COVID-19 pandemic accelerated this evolutionary process, responding to the need to conduct a design sprint that could really meet the needs of remote collaboration when necessary.

## Transition from Waterfall to Agile to Lean

I am fortunate to have begun working in the technology space at a time when waterfall was still very popular, but on its way out. Of course, even agile processes have changed over recent years, expanding primarily from Scrum and Kanban methodologies, to include Lean Development, Crystal and Extreme Programming *(XP)*. For those not familiar with the term waterfall, it's a concept closely related to design thinking. In waterfall methodology, software is not released until it's *"done."* Notably, the definition of *"done"* is unique to every organization's standards on what is acceptable for the software to launch and start having your customers use it. In waterfall, this often meant working on a new version for a year or more before it was released to clients, a software package filled with new features to please both customers or the organizations they may work for. Waterfall, much like design thinking, became challenging for many technology organizations. Outside of hot fixes or quick releases to fix bugs, a majority of features, after researching the problem you are working to solve, could take months or years to have a solution ready for your clients. The transition from waterfall to agile in itself was a significant process shift. I worked for a prominent technology firm in the document imaging space that put tremendous focus into the quality of its research and development department. Engineers were well-educated and often had to pass many tests to join the team. Product managers from various industry backgrounds were brought in as subject matter experts to spend months traveling to customer sites to understand user problems before writing requirements for the engineering team. The UX and design teams were trusted to create the best experience for users, and the operations team was the glue to making sure customer feedback and releases stayed on track for each product release, large and small. Most members of the organization were seasoned and had worked in waterfall processes for most of their careers. The shift to agile was not liked at first by many. We brought in a third party consulting firm to help shift the messaging, and with my agile tiger team assigned to the task at hand, I spearheaded training for the transition to agile processes for the operations, product, UX, design and engineering teams. We migrated much of our open bugs, user stories and tasks to Rally Software, now owned by CA technologies. I had the opportunity to administer the system and take the lead as a ScrumMaster for three development teams. We implemented a process whereby teams learned to manage their tasks in the vernacular of t-shirt sizes: x-small, small, medium, large and x-large rather than measuring in the metric of hours that we had been using for years. This change management took about 18 months to get the 150+ members of the R&D team fully transitioned from waterfall to agile, using mainly Scrum methodologies and some Kanban for the 21 engineering teams we had working on different products and solutions.

I'm reflecting on this transition from waterfall to agile as an analogy relative to the evolutionary process design thinking has undergone, whittling down from five day design sprints to two hour design sprints. In a similar fashion, design sprints have gone through the same process of enhancing processes that work best for different technology organizations. While two hour design sprints may not work best for every organization, the boost in efficiency, productivity and time savings make it worthwhile for many organizations to give it a go. From there, organizations have the experience and exposure under their belts to choose which approach best fits their needs. The result may be a hybrid of using five day design sprints for larger problems and two hour design sprints for smaller problems.

## Five Day Design Sprint Schedule

If you're not familiar with the five day design sprint schedule, keep in mind this methodology dedicates one full day to each step. Here is an example schedule, modeled after *Sprint*,[5] from one of the most recent five day design sprints I moderated.

**Day 1 - Understand**

Setup *(30 minutes)*
Breakfast and Coffee *(30 minutes)*
Moderator Introduction *(5 minutes)*
Review Design Sprint Schedule and Rules *(15 minutes)*
Share Opportunity & Research with Group *(30 minutes)*
What We Know About the Problem *(45 minutes)*
Who are the Users *(30 minutes)*
Define or Modify User Personas *(30 minutes)*
What Don't We Know about the Problem *(45 minutes)*

Lunch *(45 minutes)*
Previous Research or Designs *(90 minutes)*
Define the Problem Statement *(60 minutes)*
Create Parking Lot *(30 minutes)*
Snack and Coffee *(15 minutes)*
Five Whys *(30 minutes)*
Prioritize Cards and Assumptions *(60 minutes)*
Cleanup and Prep for Next Day *(45 minutes)*

**Day 2 - Ideate**
Setup *(30 minutes)*
Breakfast and Coffee *(30 minutes)*
Review Design Sprint Schedule and Rules *(15 minutes)*
Share Modified Opportunity & Research with Group *(30 minutes)*
Narrow Down User Personas *(60 minutes)*
Divide Up User Personas to Groups and Create Workflow *(60 minutes)*
Demo Each User Persona Workflow *(45 minutes)*
Challenge and Opportunity Statements *(60 minutes)*
Lunch *(45 minutes)*
Brainstorm and Explore Opportunities *(120 minutes)*
Crazy Eights *(60 minutes)*
Snack and Coffee *(15 minutes)*
Storyboard *(90 minutes)*
Cleanup and Prep for Next Day *(45 minutes)*

**Day 3 - Define**
Setup *(30 minutes)*
Breakfast and Coffee *(30 minutes)*
Review Design Sprint Schedule and Rules *(15 minutes)*
Share Modified Opportunity and Research with Group *(30 minutes)*

Conflict Resolution *(60 minutes)*
Review and Modify Parking Lot Items *(60 minutes)*
Quick Test Assumptions *(60 minutes)*
Lunch *(45 minutes)*
Finalize Sketching and Storyboarding *(120 minutes)*
Finalize and Update Workflows *(45 minutes)*
Agree on Storyboarding *(60 minutes)*
Snack and Coffee *(15 minutes)*
Prep for Prototype *(60 minutes)*
Cleanup and Prep for Next Day *(45 minutes)*

**Day 4 - Prototype**
Setup *(30 minutes)*
Breakfast and Coffee *(30 minutes)*
Review Design Sprint Schedule and Rules *(15 minutes)*
Share Modified Opportunity and Research with Group *(30 minutes)*
Discuss Options for Prototyping *(30 minutes)*
Low Fidelity Prototypes by User Personas *(120 minutes)*
Prototype Review and Knowledge Share *(120 minutes)*
Lunch *(45 minutes)*
Cleanup and Prep for Next Day *(45 minutes)*
Vote on Prototypes *(30 minutes)*
Higher Fidelity Prototypes by User Personas *(150 minutes)*
Snack and Coffee *(15 minutes)*
Prep and Finalize Prototypes to Test *(60 minutes)*
Confirm Users for Testing Tomorrow *(30 minutes)*
Cleanup and Prep for Next Day *(45 minutes)*

**Day 5 - Test**
Setup *(30 minutes)*
Breakfast and Coffee *(30 minutes)*
Review Design Sprint Schedule and Rules *(15 minutes)*

Share Final Opportunity and Research with Group *(30 minutes)*
Discuss Goals for the Day in Testing *(30 minutes)*
Finalize Testing Plan, Questions and Prototype Review *(60 minutes)*
User Testing, at least 5 Users per User Persona *(180 minutes)*
Lunch *(45 minutes)*
Agree on Assumptions and Changes as Group *(30 minutes)*
Review Parking Lot and Determine Next Steps *(30 minutes)*
Agree on Business Opportunity and User Case *(60 minutes)*
Discuss whether we Solved the Problem with our Solution *(30 minutes)*
Determine Next Steps for Design Changes or Needs *(30 minutes)*

In a nutshell, each day boils down to this:
Day 1 – Understand
Day 2 – Ideate
Day 3 – Define
Day 4 – Prototype
Day 5 – Test

Notice there's a time box for each line item on the agenda for the day, down to 15 minute increments. One of the challenges I've experienced with five day design sprints is getting through the material with a large group of stakeholders in the time allotment. It's also a very long day – every day for five consecutive days – and oftentimes attendees are not able to stay the full five days which means you might not be problem-solving in the way you intended. I know I'm guilty of having to pop out for client meetings, phone calls or to check emails during week-long design sprints. It is very challenging to dedicate a full five days of attention to problem solving when you're juggling several responsibilities and managing daily tasks in an organization. In addition, if you are using design sprints to solve every single problem or issue, it's unrealistic to expect a group of stakeholders to participate in design sprints all day long. Perhaps an organization as large as Google[6] with more than 187,000 employees may have that bandwidth, however, 99% of tech firms in the United States have less than 500 employees, according to Wonder.[7] The value of two hour design sprints is not only solving more problems in a shorter amount of time, but also not straining the group of stakeholders you need feedback from in the process.

## Five Day Design Sprint Challenges

Five day design sprints do not adapt well to remote collaboration. I recall the first design sprint I sought to run via Zoom[8] when COVID-19 reached the United States and the lockdowns began in March 2020. Our organization was 100% remote and our team was looking to explore an analytics solution that could predict the habits of customers. To say the least, it was a challenging task. It would have been ineffective, if not impossible, to conduct a three- or two-day design sprint and keep the attention of everyone on Zoom. Although certainly useful, particularly when conducted in person to collaborate on solutions for complex problems, the five biggest limitations of five day design sprints are:

- Too expensive

- Not friendly for remote collaboration

- Hard to get key stakeholders in a room for the full five days

- Loss of productive time from the team

- Additional design sprints are sometimes needed

# My Last Five Day Design Sprint

The last five day design sprint I participated in was challenging, so much so that a second five day design sprint was needed, and then a third, costing the organization thousands of dollars and hours of lost productivity. This experience was a big driver for me to explore faster methods for problem-solving. The shortened time frame is not meant to cut corners, but to target the root causes of a problem using an operational approach instead of a five day analytical session. If two hour design sprints had been an available tool at our disposal, we could have saved three weeks spent by employees, stakeholders and customers.

At the time, design sprints were the hot new method being used by Silicon Valley technology companies due to the popularity and expertise of Google and GV. We brought in a third party to run our first two five day design sprints, and we ran it internally for the third and final one. Although design sprints were not a new concept to the organization, they did not have an easy path to executive buy-in. It took months of research from several teammates to convince the executive team to bring in a third party to lead design sprints with a price tag of nearly $50,000 and a contract that committed us to at least three design sprints over the next 12-18 months. While I was not the facilitator for the new product features being discussed, I was a key stakeholder. I remember the very first day we all fit into a tiny conference room, with not enough seats to go around. Of course, this set-up was pre-COVID-19 with no worries about how closely we were all crammed together.

**Day 1:** Most of the first day was used as an introduction to the concept of design sprints. The facilitator spelled out the ground rules *(no technology was allowed)*, explained what everyone's role was and why it was important to attend the entire session. This entire day's agenda could have been condensed to mere minutes.

The atmosphere in the room was positive but dull as the process was laid out to all stakeholders. Several stakeholders raised their hand and mentioned they had critical client meetings they would need to attend and hopped back and forth throughout the week, ignoring the ground rules that dictated no laptops or cell phones for the week.

**Day 2:** We spent the second day mapping the customer journey and narrowing down user personas. We split into groups to each take a different persona and think through the user cases. Below is an example of one of the personas, Austin the Analyst *(see Figure 3.2)*. You'll notice the detail in creating goals, frustrations, wants, dream scenarios and demographics for his role as an analyst.

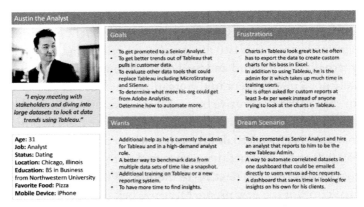

*Figure 3.2*

**Day 3:** We began storyboarding and looking at what problems we would be solving for users. We had three groups and each group defined problems for their respective personas. What made this day increasingly difficult was opposing perspectives on what we thought users wanted versus what they would actually use if they had it in the product. Here is an example of the workflow storytelling each group created for their respective personas *(see figure 3.3)*.

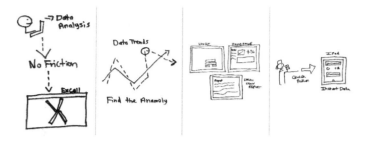

*Figure 3.3*

**Day 4:** Now that we thought we understood the personas, customer journeys, and problems, we began to sketch out ideas that would be needed the next day for each persona. In theory, this step would prepare us for 15 customer sessions on day five. We would need five users for each of the three personas. This is really where the wheels started coming off the bus. Solutioning for three personas was too much of a commitment to get in front of clients the next day, and even though the designer and I stayed up until 2 a.m. working on designs, we agreed as a team to only share the work for one of the three personas.

**Day 5:** The original schedule planned to test five customers for each of the three personas *(15 customer interview sessions).* As two of the personas were unable to be completed, we continued to review the designs with five customers for one persona. Only three of the five scheduled customers showed up, and of the three we did interview, one of the stakeholders sent over another employee from their team, which did not match the persona for which we were interviewing. In a nutshell, it was a bit of a hot mess.

**Retrospective:** As we were an agile shop, we conducted a retrospective including the third party moderator and determined that this problem was too large to solve with a five day design sprint. We decided we needed to dedicate one five day design sprint for each persona.

**Day 6-Day 15:** We conducted two more five day design sprints for the remaining two personas. What we ended up learning is that the other two personas would never have been users of the product. So, the designs and budget for these personas were thrown out entirely. At the end of the day, this was a very costly exercise for which we could have avoided by learning that earlier in the process as you would during a two hour design sprint.

CHAPTER 4

# *HISTORY OF UX*

In Chapter 3, *"Evolution of the Design Sprint"* we discussed how the concept of design thinking and design sprints have continued to evolve over time dating back to the 1970s and 1980s. The concept of User Experience *(UX)* which encompasses the full spectrum of ways the user interacts with products, services or experiences dates back even further.

## The Design of Everyday Things by Don Norman

The author and cognitive scientist Don Norman is known for his book *The Design of Everyday Things,* first published in 1980. He is said to have coined the term *"user experience"* in 1993 while working at Apple Computer. To the contrary, the field of UX was launched in the 1950s, according to the Nielsen Norman Group,[1] where Bell Labs performed UX during the creation of a new keypad. Now seven decades later, the Nielsen Norman Group projects the number of UX professionals around the world will continue to grow by a factor of 100, from one million in 2017 to 100 million in 2050. Its projections span a century from 1950 to 2050.

## The rise of UX in Technology Organizations

Throughout my career in software technology companies, the level of UX investment in my professional experience has varied. For example, I've worked for companies with fewer than 1,000 employees that invested significant resources to build a strong UX team consisting of designers, researchers, and front-end developers to influence and shape the product. I've also worked for companies employing more than 10,000 people that did not commit resources to build a dedicated UX team; instead they chose to rely on the product management team to fill the UX role. In my experience, the decision to invest in a core UX team yields tangible and intangible benefits. And it correlates with the mission of the organization. Does it place a priority on improving experiences for the end-user, the customer? I've had the opportunity to help build UX teams from the ground up at three organizations. Each wanted to dedicate a team to enhance the user experience. My professional experience with UX investment at these organizations supports the projections of the Nielsen Group.

## 2000-2010

Early in my career, the company I was working for had more than 10,000 employees. It was exploring steps to invest in a dedicated UX team. While UX was very important, much of the UX role lived within the product management team. As the company looked into boosting its UX team, it took a deep dive into Customer Experience *(CX)* data.

## UX vs. CX

UX and CX are processes often used in a technology organization, depending upon which constituency it is serving. According to usabilitygeek.com, the meanings may be defined this way: *"UX focuses on the end user while CX focuses on the customer."*[2] At this larger technology company, I started as an analyst on the product team and often crossed over into CX and UX data to examine user behavioral metrics. Perhaps this is what later piqued my interest in guiding and managing UX teams later in my career. I examined feedback and comments from customers using Clarabridge, acquired by Qualtrics in 2021,[3] an AI-driven tool that was in its infancy to identify data trends but yet advanced enough to help influence decisions we would make for our products. The product I was working on at the time was transitioning users moving from physical software packaging to digital software. Customer feedback was crucial to build the right features that would support the shift in the market towards digital software packaging. In this instance, the organization did not have a dedicated UX team but was able to leverage the product and CX teams to solve problems experienced by users in the product.

## 2010-2020

In this decade, I worked for an up-and-coming technology firm that experienced explosive growth, nearly doubling its workforce during each of the four and a half years of my employment. As we transitioned from waterfall to agile methodologies, we adapted our processes to focus two large scrum teams on UX, including researchers, designers and front-end developers. They were tasked to create the best experience with the product, conducting usability testing and workflow enhancement across devices. In addition, we invested in a CX team to create a forum for customers to provide feedback about their experiences with the product, share wants and needs, and rank NPS *(Net Promoter Score)*.

By using NPS the teams increased customer shadowing, onsite visits and customer surveys. I had the opportunity to work for and with both of these teams and initiatives as well as in product management, and this was by far the biggest shift in investment I have seen at a technology organization, with major payoffs in its success.

## Net Promoter Score

If you are not familiar with the concept of NPS, it is a measurement of customer experience created by Satmetrix[4] with whom I received my Certified Net Promoter Certification in 2010. NPS is a great measurement to take a pulse on the likelihood of your customers recommending your products to their friends or colleagues. In addition to a score on a 10-point scale, customers are able to leave valuable feedback in open-ended comments that could help drive significant product development for your organization. If you are not using NPS as part of your UX strategy today, you should. Not only have I implemented NPS at every organization I have worked for the past 15+ years, I use it to drive organizational buy-in through its powerful collection of user feedback in addition to scores. I highly recommend and have implemented during the course of my career Medallia,[5] Salesforce,[6] Service Management Group,[7] Qualtrics,[8] and SurveyMonkey[9] for smaller organizations that do not have the budget for an enterprise solution.

# 2020-Present

The organization I work for today, TreviPay, believes so strongly in the value of UX and CX that empathy is even integral to our mission statement. I am fortunate to be a leader for product management, user experience, and design. Using this platform,

I strive to create the best experiences for our clients and their users. Our product team has more than 25 team members, and our UX and design teams have doubled in size with nearly 10 members respectively since I started working here in 2018. As we continue to grow our client base and solution offerings, I expect these teams to grow even more.

## Budget for UX Varies

Overall, I have seen different levels of investment across each organization I have worked for in nearly two decades immersed in the technology sector. The amount of time and money an organization is willing to invest in UX directly impacts the methods used, including design thinking and design sprints. A large organization does not necessarily equal a large UX team or large budget to conduct research. Likewise, many small organizations invest with a customer-first mindset and they prioritize UX. In 2018, I got a glimpse of an organization that had the largest investment in UX I have seen in my career. I accepted an interview to be a leader for its UX team, which had more than 150 employees and 10 levels of hierarchy in its U.S. office alone. This organization took the trendy approach that Meta was known for by creating hierarchy in its management ranks to explore growth, one that helped promote additional hiring during the COVID-19 pandemic and increase in remote workforce.[10] I can only imagine in 2023 they are having the same struggles as many technology organizations are in a post-pandemic economy to determine whether they need to downsize staff. Mark Zuckerberg, co-founder and CEO of Meta has called 2023 the *"year of efficiency"*[11] and is flattening Meta's structure by *"removing some layers of middle management."* While two hour design sprints won't determine whether layoffs are imminent, it can help provide organizations with additional opportunities for growth in UX, grow the roadmap and make happier clients to help grow your business.

## UX & Automation - Boomers, Gen X, Millennials, Gen Z

As we look at the continued investment in UX at technology organizations, one must ask the question, what is driving the explosive growth in UX? While Don Norman coined the term UX decades ago, the type of products available since then has drastically shifted. Coming of age in the United States in the 90s, including many Gen Xers *(1965-1980)* and Millenials *(1981-1996)*[12] did not mean growing up with instant gratification at one's fingertips like the generations today, including Generation Z *(1997-2012)* and Generation Alpha *(2010-2024)*.[13] While it came close in 1991 with the release of Super Nintendo in the U.S. *(and as Super Famicom in Japan in 1990)*,[14] it took years for new releases in a series to come out, including some of my all-time favorites: Super Mario World *(1990)*, Super Mario Kart *(1992)*, and Super Mario World 2 *(1995)*.[15] In fact, UX was the biggest driver for an entirely different console in the U.S. thanks to Nintendo's U.S. designer, Lance Barr. That can be credited to major competition in the market thanks to the release and popularity of the Sega Genesis in 1988.[16] New game and product releases for game series today happen at a much faster pace, and the options for what and how gamers choose to play are endless. Not only are users able to choose the game they want to play, but on which device - PC, Mac, XBox, PlayStation, Wii, Switch, Nintendo, iPad, iPhone, Fire, the list goes on. Each of these devices is a different UX pending one's needs as the user, unlike in the 90s when the main competition between Super Nintendo and Sega Genesis was limited to a handful of devices, including the Nintendo Gameboy, which released in 1989.[17] The increased need for UX is driven by the increased number of experiences available to consumers, across all generations. While we have focused on gaming, the urgent need for innovation and better user experience applies to nearly every consumer experience imaginable, from social media, to streaming services, apps and more. There has been a generational shift in how we access what we need in our daily lives. Long gone are the days of convincing your sibling to hang up the phone so you can log in to AOL Instant Messenger and chat with your friends. While Wi-Fi was invented in 1997, it was not in 25% of homes worldwide until 2012, according to Fon.[18] As we continue to automate solutions for users, we increase the need to do so across all platforms and avenues of life. Two hour design sprints respond to the demand to solve problems faster and more efficiently. This allows organizations to release solutions and products to customers faster than the competition and delivers what today's customers and end users have become accustomed to – instant gratification at their fingertips.

**CHAPTER 5**

# *IMPACT OF REMOTE WORK ON DESIGN SPRINTS*

Even prior to the COVID-19 pandemic, remote work in the technology sector was becoming more common. However, not every organization embraced the concept. I've had several leaders in my career who opposed remote work and whose organizations implemented policies disallowing remote work altogether. Before COVID-19 disrupted life as we knew it, running a remote design sprint was not a typical undertaking. It was widely believed that it would be more effective to have everyone participate in person, even if that meant flying in international stakeholders to attend. Five day design sprints could certainly be done remotely, but in-person engagement is part of the success in the design sprint concept created by Jake Knapp and the team at GV. I talked a bit about my story regarding some of the challenges I experienced when pandemic-related shutdowns forced our organization to tackle a problem while working remotely. It was imperative to conduct and complete a design sprint for a critical business problem that involved scoring customers who were not paying their bills. I immediately began to research how others were performing virtual design sprints and found nothing. So, I decided to modify the process I had learned over the years from design thinking concepts, consulting firms and books on design sprints inspired by Jake Knapp and the team at GV Ventures. Through trial and error, I modified the in-person concept to a virtual format that allowed our organization to survive and thrive through the uncertainties created by pandemic-related shutdowns. I pioneered virtual problem-solving workshops at TreviPay that have lasting utility, as our organization continued to stay remote even after shutdown restrictions were lifted. It dawned on me that other technology organizations certainly were experiencing similar challenges to evolve or dissolve in the current work environment. Remote and hybrid work arrangements are here to stay for the foreseeable future, so perhaps the concept of two hour design sprints is too. This led me down the path of speaking at conferences and workshops about virtual design sprints to help other organizations reap the benefits of this modified approach as well.

## Solving Big Problems with No Budget

In addition to the challenges of adapting to remote work arrangements, many organizations cut funding and jobs in 2019 due to the pandemic. If you have not had the opportunity to run one or get approval for one, five day design sprints are very expensive. Some even require a built-in budget to accommodate from one year to the next. Even if you don't bring in a consulting firm to run your five day design sprint – which could cost anywhere from $10,000-$100,000 – there's financial and productivity considerations to have 20 team members spend 40+ hours in a room together for five full work days. Let's take a look at what it would cost an organization to have 20 team members spend five full days in a room together. The average median pay for a Google employee was $246,804 in 2018[1] or roughly $123.40/ hour per employee. This would mean if Google had 20 employees participate in one five day design sprint just once in 2018, it would cost $98,720, and that cost does not include the cost of food. Google is known for great free food perks for its employees.[2] Imagine if Google, an organization with nearly 187,000 employees in 2022[3] had 1% of its employee base *(1,870 employees)* run just one design sprint per year. That would be roughly 94 design sprints and would cost Google $9,279,680. Do the math: *94 design sprints x $98,720 cost per design sprint, based on the hourly rate of $123.40/employee, using the median Google salary per employee of $246, 804.* Design sprints are still the primary method for kickstarting projects today at Google[4] and many of the groups Jake Knapp worked with had ***"an appetite for five or ten design sprints a year,"[5]*** including up to 50 stakeholders at a time. This would more than quadruple our original cost estimates for an organization like Google to run design sprints. While not every organization has the budget or payroll the size of Google, even using a smaller hourly rate shows what it would cost your organization to run just one five day design sprint *(see Figure 5.1).*

## Employee Cost to Run a Five Day Design Sprint

**Hourly Rate x # Employees x Hours in a five day design sprint = Organizational Cost**

$50/hr x 20 employees x 40 hours = $40,000 to run one five day design sprint

$75/hr x 20 employees x 40 hours = $60,000 to run one five day design sprint

$100/hr x 20 employees x 40 hours = $80,000 to run one five day design sprint

*Google's $123.40/hr x 20 employees x 40 hours = $98,720 to run one five day design sprint*

$125/hr x 20 employees x 40 hours = $100,000 to run one five day design sprint

*Figure 5.1*

Keep in mind, salary averages could be higher or lower depending on the organization. This cost analysis also does not include the time spent to prepare for a five day design sprint. For example, the moderator duties would probably add at least another 10-20 hours beforehand and up to 40 hours following the design sprint. Organizations that needed to trim their budgets during the pandemic likely still needed a multi-day design sprint to identify and solve problems. So, it required thinking outside the box to make things work. I know other organizations made similar modifications to the design sprint process when their workforce went remote. However, even now that we are back at the office full-time, we are still using the two hour design sprint process, whether virtual or in person. The efficiencies and success we achieved with two hour design sprints eliminate the need to go back to a five day design sprint model. I've had the opportunity to coach many organizations globally on this concept, and will walk through some success stories on moving to a two hour design sprint model in place of or in addition to five day design sprints in Chapter 14: *"Two Hour Design Sprint Success Stories."*

## A Hybrid Approach

Two hour design sprints are inspired by a hybrid methodology derived from the Stanford d.School[6] method on design thinking as well as five day design sprints developed by Jake Knapp and the team from GV.[7] The two hour design sprint method focuses on two segments, what you might call the Alpha and the Omega. Alpha: Three stages during the design sprint. Omega: Two stages after the design sprint is completed. We will go into more detail on the benefits of these two segments and examine why it works well with the process. First, we'll take a look at the methodology in the hybrid approach. The first three stages during the design sprint *(Alpha)* focuses on empathizing with customers, exploring the problem and ideating solutions. The next phase *(Omega)* focuses on prototyping solutions and testing with customers after the design sprint is completed *(Figure 5.2)*.

*Figure 5.2*

## During the Two Hour Design Sprint

Here is how a typical two hour design sprint schedule looks in the first three stages: empathizing with customers, exploring the problem and ideating solutions.

### *Alpha*

**Empathize with Customers (30 Minutes)**
- Review Agenda & Rules *(5 minutes)*

- Quick Figma FigJam Overview *(5 minutes)*
- Review Customer Understandings & User Personas *(20 minutes)*

**Explore the Problem (40 Minutes)**
- Finalize Problem Statement as a Group *(10 minutes)*
- Questions and Storyboard Brainstorm *(30 minutes)*

**Ideate Solutions (50 Minutes)**
- Low Fidelity Sketching *(20 minutes)*
- Present Low Fidelity Designers *(20 minutes)*
- Vote on Sketches *(5 minutes)*
- Next Steps *(5 minutes)*

All three stages are condensed to 120 minutes, reducing the time frame from three days *(one day per stage)* used in a traditional five day design sprint. The condensed schedule focuses on the core details necessary to have the strongest impact for problem solving. In the first stage – empathizing with customers – the most productive schedule is to review the agenda, talk a bit about any collaborative whiteboard tools you will be using such as Figma FigJam and review the customer understandings and personas. In the second stage – exploring the problem – you will create a problem statement as a group, storyboard, and ask more questions. In the final stage of the two hour hour design sprint – ideating solutions – some may wonder if there is time for sketching. I can confirm there absolutely is time to sketch in this stage and it happens to be my favorite stage of a design sprint. It is critical for a successful outcome. As a group, each team member gets to present individual solutions before voting.

# After the Two Hour Design Sprint

Here is what a typical schedule looks like *after* the two hour design sprint in the final two stages: prototype solutions and test with customers. We will discuss more in Chapter 9: *"Stage 4 & 5 Prototype and Test"* why these stages are more successful outside of the two hour design sprint process.

### *Omega*

**Prototype Solutions *(150 Minutes)***
- High Fidelity Designs *(90 Minutes)*
- Build Prototype *(60 Minutes)*

**Test with Customers *(150 Minutes)***
- Testing with Users *(90 Minutes)*
- Review Testing Feedback *(30 Minutes)*

A key difference between two hour design sprints and traditional five day design sprints is the recommendation to conduct prototyping and testing outside of the two hour design sprint process. In a traditional five day design sprint, two full days are dedicated to prototype and test. Two hour design sprints allow you to control the amount of time defining and solving a problem for users and not put all your eggs in one basket. Even with a five day design sprint, more design changes and testing are often needed, even after you've already spent a full five days on the design sprint. So, why not simplify and streamline the process? Save time and resources. Committing to a two hour design sprint eliminates many of the headaches and challenges that come with cramming everything in one week.

## Technology Replaces In-Person Collaboration

A key ingredient needed to successfully implement two hour design sprints is the collaborative digital tools available to support the remote transition. While collaborative tools for digital whiteboards such as InVision[8] and Miro[9] have been adding new features over the years, including the release of Figma FigJam[10] in beta in 2021,[11] the adoption of these tools accelerated during the pandemic, much like the adoption of Zoom[12] for video collaboration.

## Two Hour Design Sprint Figma FigJam Template

You will hear me talk a lot about Figma FigJam as I am a big fan of its collaborative whiteboard feature and have been using it since it was only in beta in 2021. However, I have and still use InVision Freehand and Miro on occasion. I have not personally used Mural[13] but I know many that have had success with it as well. Adobe was scheduled to acquire Figma for $20 billion on September 17, 2022[14] however, at the time of publication of this book, the government was discussing whether to block the Adobe absorption of Figma over monopoly fears.[15] If the acquisition goes through, I'm curious to see whether Adobe will continue to operate the software as its own division or move Figma and the product Figma FigJam into the Adobe user licensing model as a new solution. I am also an active Adobe Creative Cloud[16] user so I would enjoy either path; I just hope Adobe continues to invest in features. See Figure 5.3 for details on a two hour design sprint Figma FigJam board I created that I will reference throughout the book. You may easily recreate this board on your own or search for it in the Figma FigJam community *"2 Hour Design Sprints"* by Teresa Cain.[17]

*Figure 5.3*

## Two Hour Design Sprint Agenda

In Chapter 5: *"Impact of Remote Work on Design Sprints,"* I reviewed a typical two hour design sprint schedule as well as the *2 Hour Design Sprints* Figma FigJam board. If you are accessing the template in the Figma FigJam community, it will show the agenda as seen in Figure 5.4. You will notice the agenda has more detail than the schedule, and walks through the steps that will be taken during each section, including Intro and Review, Empathize with Customers, Explore the Problem, Ideate Solutions, Presentation, Group Voting of Ideate Solutions, and Workshop Summary & Next Steps.

**Agenda**

**Intro and Review (5 minutes)**
- Discuss the 2 hour design sprint process.

**Empathize with Customers (25 minutes)**
- Review current pain points, needs and observations of users.
- Storyboard and add to sticky notes individually.
- Vote as individuals using stamps on top three pain points for end-users.

**Explore the Problem (30 minutes)**
- "How might we?" exercise - frame a challenge into a question. How might we solve a problem that has been defined?
- Storyboard and add to sticky notes individually.
- Vote as individuals using stamps on top three problem explorations for end-users.

**Ideate Solutions (30 minutes)**
- Sketching exercise for visualizing potential solution.
- Work individually to explore the problem – free form using paper or Figma or any tool to draw or convey.

**Presentation (20 minutes)**
- All attendees gets 1-2 minutes to present the value prop of their sketch and solution to the problem.

**Group Voting of Ideate Solutions (5 minutes)**
- Vote as individuals using stamps on top three solutions for end-users.

**Workshop Summary & Next Steps (5 minutes)**
- We will take a few minutes to talk about the top two designs and opportunity to move forward as a group with prototyping and testing with customers.

*Figure 5.4*

I encourage you to use a timer for each of these sections. The built-in timer in Figma FigJam works quite well and will keep you on track and on task for your two hour design sprint. You may also use a timer on your phone or any other device.

# *INTERLUDE: THE IMPORTANCE OF DISCOVERY RE-SEARCH BEFORE THE TWO HOUR DESIGN SPRINT BY JOHN KILLE*

## Why UX Research?

One of the most important pieces for conducting an effective two hour design sprint is the prep work. In short, you get out what you put in. As you begin to prep, take into account the problem as a whole. More than a decade ago, Jake Knapp and team at then-Google Ventures created the design sprint method as a way of exploring and solving a problem in a short amount of time – as he describes in his book *Sprint: How to Solve Big Problems and Test New Ideas in Just Five Days.*[1] Shortening the collaboration time dramatically with design sprint participants from five days to just two hours requires advance work. Prep is a crucial piece of the puzzle to successful problem solving. You will need evidence to showcase how the problem came about and what the current users or potential users are experiencing – the what and the why. In my career as a UX researcher and designer, I've explored a variety of learning methods to further understand human behaviors, issues, and problems to help create solutions. A central aspect of solutioning rests in how clearly you and your team understand the problem. In this interlude, I will discuss the importance of UX discovery research prior to conducting the two hour design sprint, as well as some methods I have used and why these methods help set up the design sprint. I will also discuss how to showcase what you have learned after conducting the discovery research, such as creating personas, to present your findings to design sprint participants. That way, your team will start on the same page with a solid understanding about the scope of the problem your design sprint is tackling so that you are best set up to achieve an effective solution.

## Methods of Understanding

As part of the set-up process for the two hour design sprint, you must first delve deeply into learning about the users and the issues they are having. As Laura Klein discusses in *UX for Lean StartUps*,[2] a sizable number of tech start-ups fail because these organizations haven't dug deep enough to identify the root problem users are confronting with their product solution. That is, if the team failed to do its research and identify the main problem users may be having with the product solution, the team is less likely to solve the specific user problems, and therefore the product fails. The non-negotiable starting point for solving problems, either big, small, or somewhere in be- tween, is first understanding the root of that problem. This is where the discovery – or understanding research – is crucial to a productive two hour design sprint experience. There are various types of research methods to explore the problem you will be trying to solve during the two hour design sprint. Some of the main variables for which method to use may include: How much time do you have to learn about the user? What is your budget? How many people are going to be conducting the research? What is your user *(or potential user)* database for learning and getting feedback? To help you get started, I will walk you through a few methods I have used in arranging Stage 1 Empathize with Customers in the two hour design sprint.

## User Interviews

The user interview is one of the basic methods of understanding a user or potential user of a product or product feature. It consists of the researcher spending 1:1 time with a user or potential user, asking a series of carefully crafted questions to learn more about their goals, needs, and pains around a particular focus. Having too broad of a focus in your questioning will yield less effective results. Keep in mind, the more focused the interview is on learning a particular behavior and discovering specific issues the user is having with the current solution will produce better intelligence to identify the scope of the problem to solve. Prior to conducting an interview, you must first craft a study guide. This is a breakdown of what the project is, the research goal or goals, which participants they will be using for the study, as well as specific questions to help learn more about the issues. Having all questions mapped out helps the team drill down to discover the root of a problem, such as user motivations and triggers, etc. The study guide also aligns all members of the team who will be learning about the user. These interviews can be conducted over the phone, using a video conferencing tool such as Zoom,[3] Microsoft Teams,[4] or conducted in person. The focus is to talk to users directly and learn from them instead of relying on secondary sources alone.

Prior to starting the interview, you must first have a focused goal that you would like to learn from your set of users. Here are some examples of research goals that I have delved into in past projects at various companies I have worked for. I will be using these examples periodically throughout the interlude:

- Learn how university teachers keep track and record students' progress during a semester, including problems they may be having with the tool and specifics they wanted the product to solve.

- Understand how an accounts payable professional receives invoices from various sources and how that individual pays those invoices. What tools are used in the process, what are the pain points with those tools and why are they causing problems?

- Learn how millennials listen to music on the go. What sources do they use and why? What are the main elements they look for in using a music app or method used to get music on the go? What do they look for in an app and why is it working or not working for their needs?

By having a focused goal you will use to formulate your questions, you can streamline the research and have multiple researchers conduct the same study. This also shortens the amount of time it takes to gain insight.

Keep in mind, you do need to stay laser-focused on the user's goals, needs, and pains in connection with your research goal. Also, you should only need to interview between four and six users or potential users to help answer your research questions. If you cannot reach this number of users, remember that interviewing one user or potential user is better than interviewing none. Likewise, interviewing three is better than two, and two is better than one because you will gain more insights about your user base. The important thing with qualitative research is insight, and the real focus is about your user set.

## Contextual Inquiry or Ethnographic Research Methods

A qualitative method rooted in the anthropology discipline, ethnographic research is conducted by meeting and learning about the users – and the problem they may be experiencing – in the environment in which they are using the product. This approach, although more time consuming and expensive, allows you to ask questions about the user's experience, in real time, in the user's environment. It also gives you the opportunity to observe cultural nuances that shape the user's experiences. For example, using one of the aforementioned research goals, spending time with individual university professors in the environment in which they are tracking and recording students' progress provides context for potential barriers, such as student inquiry and disruptions, overloaded course loads and high student-to-faculty ratios, and/or outdated technology that may impact performance. These on-site insights add more color and important context to the data gathered than an offsite or remote interview would provide.

Similar to the sample size when conducting interviews, a small sample size is ideal for this type of research as well. Ethnographic research is rooted in the philosophy that *"everything is data,"* – i.e., all sensory information the researcher hears, sees, smells, etc. is part of the user experience. Taking this into account will enhance the information you learn. Understanding the users in their own environment adds value to the interview process and improves the findings of the research.

## Surveys

Another method that can be used to examine users prior to the design sprint is to create and implement a survey. If resources are limited, surveys can reach a wider variety of users or potential users in a shorter amount of time than individual interviews. Also, they are less expensive to implement. For example, sending an email to your user group takes fewer resources than investing in in-person interviews. Be mindful, however, that the survey method provides limited *"follow-up questions"* that the interview process allows. So, the data produced is not as rich and insightful. However, this approach still offers insight about the set of users and adds to the bank of understanding-centered research. Be strategic with your questions. Asking questions that allow the user to answer quickly, but effectively, is crucial here. For higher completion rates, first advise the user how much time the survey will take. You should also explain the survey's purpose and share why completed surveys will provide mutually beneficial results to improve user experience with the product. That way, the participant knows what to expect and is more likely to participate.

## Behavioral Data and Clickstream Analysis

If you are exploring issues related to elements of the user experience that users are currently experiencing, then delving into the behavioral data can help with user understanding and identify the scope of the issue. This method requires a configured setup, such as Google Analytics[5], Amplitude[6], Lucky Orange[7], Hot Jar[8], or other similar tools that capture what the users are looking at, what pages they are visiting or not visiting, and time spent on various pages. Analyzing what users are currently doing – or not doing – within a product feature is highly informative research. For example, you may discover they are not visiting the portion of the site you want them to visit. So, you may learn when and where they may be dropping out of the site. This is lucrative information to digest. Note the data from Google Analytics *(or a similar tool)* demonstrates genuine user behavior – it provides the unvarnished truth as to what users are doing and how many are doing it. To effectively fix a problem, you need to know its scope. Is it just a few users or a majority of your user base? Is it a certain segment of users experiencing the same thing? Using information from clickstream analytics will show your design sprint participants what the users are currently doing and how many are doing it. The data and raw numbers will complement what you have learned in the interviews. The qualitative information, such as the interviews – whether in-person, via video streaming tool or over the phone – will inform you of the why.

## What Do I Do with All of These Discoveries and Understandings?

After learning from your users, the next step is to package what you learned. Then, insert this summary into the Figma FigJam template[9] section *"Stage 1: Empathize with/Understand Customers,"* so that it is easily digestible for the participants. As Teresa will discuss in this book, the initial 20 minutes of a two hour design sprint is dedicated to the moderators presenting not only the problem statement, but also what is known about the users and why the problem is present. What are the users' current methods to solve primary problems? What are their pains and workarounds to combat those pains? What issues do they anticipate they may need help solving? What are they currently experiencing in the current feature or application that may be used to solve the issue?

### Present for Quick Learning

Presenting all of the discoveries in the design sprint canvas can sometimes be a challenge, since you may have more information than you can present in 20 minutes. You will need to be selective regarding which learnings you believe will have the most impact on your design sprint participants. For example, what is the current user experience you will be exploring? What are users' goals they are trying to achieve with the current solution? How well does the solution align to their goals? What are some needs they expressed in the interviews? What are some current pains they may be having with the current solution and to what level are these pains?

## Show Information that is Relevant to Your Problem Statement

If you have access to Net Promoter Score *(NPS)*[10] values pertaining to the current solution or behavioral data/clickstream analysis, select which parts of this information can help tell the overall story that demonstrates evidence of your problem statement. For example, let's go back to my example about professors keeping track of student progress. You may have learned in your interviews that your users find high value in entering specific grades. However, you can see in the clickstream analysis that the segment of the software designed to allow professors to enter grades is underutilized. Marrying the two data pieces may identify a need to redesign that particular feature of the product. Blending these two data points – *"what are my users doing"* and *"why are they doing it"* – gleaned from interviews or ethnographic research findings will help your design sprint participants take into account the full picture. And that will help your team brainstorm and collaborate more effectively during the two hour design sprint.

## Package User Learnings into Personas for Easy Understanding

Another way to provide your design sprint participants information on the user group is to package your findings from the interviews and clickstream analysis into personas. A persona is a concise document that summarizes and visualizes a group of people or users as one synthesized, fictional person or user.

Software designer and engineer extraordinaire, Alan Cooper, coined the term in his 1999 book, *The Inmates are Running the Asylum*,[11] and explained why channeling a user group into a fictionalized person can help product creators visualize users in a more direct way. Essentially, stakeholders identify better with the fictionalized persona, and make a closer connection to the user's goals, needs, and pains when they empathize with the user as a real human. A persona attempts to answer questions such as, *"Who are we building for?"* and *"What features or functions will empower our potential users?"* Packaging user-learning research into personas will help your design sprint participant focus on the goals, needs, and pains of the user and potential user.

## Creating the Persona

Creating personas can be something you tackle in-house, or you can hire a UX consultant to help create them. To create a persona, take your learnings from your interviews, clickstream analytics, and in-app feedback data and synthesize them. Your goal is to create the fictionalized person with four categories that drills down on the motivations of the user groups:

Demographics: This is a synthesis of who the user group generally represents and how it relates to the product. For example, age, internet use, knowledge of your product, average time on your product, social network use, etc.

Goals: What are the main things the user wants to do in relation to your product, as well as tertiary goals?

Needs: What are some of the items users need to achieve their goals, but are lacking?

Pains: What are some items preventing users from achieving their goals?

Centering the persona on motivations of the user group is the most important part of the process. What goal is the user trying to achieve and how does the product help or hinder users from achieving this goal? The persona, or personas, depending on who the problem is affecting, will allow your design sprint participants to focus attention on who the user is and understand the behaviors and engagement with the software. It will provide your design sprint participants with a visual marker for whom they are working to create a solution and why. Finally, make sure you create a clever name for the persona and have a picture *(use a free picture site)* to make the persona more human.

## Existing Personas

If you, or other members of your team, have already created personas, this is great. You can use these for your design sprint. If created well, they should offer insight to your user group. However, it is important to review and make sure the goals, pains, and needs of the persona still match the user group with whom you're currently working. As a general rule, update personas every six months to a year to keep them fresh. As society moves and technologies progress, personas need to be updated to stay current with cultural changes and users' adaptations to product features. After all, the persona is a basic but essential piece of user experience research. It helps us move into the minds of our users *(and potential users)*, listen to who they are, and understand their needs, wants, and emotions. By creating solid personas, making them available to your design sprint participants, and updating them periodically, you will have one more tool in your kit to help craft user-friendly product designs.

# Conclusion: Successful Design Sprint Prep

After you have performed the research and determined which data to showcase to help tell the story during Stage 1 Empathize with Customers of the two hour design sprint, now it's time to prep your work to present. Arrange it on the Figma FigJam template[12] that will help you show the story, i.e., why the current problem is occurring. For example, you may arrange the personas first to show the design sprint participants who the current users are. List their goals, motivations, and current pains. List solutions they may have mentioned to address some of the pains. Then, list your clickstream analytics to help showcase what users are doing with the product. Share the most important findings of the interviews. What information best addresses the problem statement the most? Let's use one of my previous examples. If you learned the accounts payable persona looks for three things in an invoice – the date the money is due, how much is due, and where the money needs to go – that explains the motivation from the user and this information should be listed prominently, particularly if this is central to the overall problem statement.

Overall, plan your research ahead of time, whether it is a two hour or five day design sprint. Planning will give you time to create a solid story for your design sprint participants. It may take one to three weeks *(or longer)* to conduct interviews, dig through clickstream analytics, gather additional feedback with other tools you may have, and compile all of your information into a workable narrative. So, keep this in mind prior to setting up the design sprint. Essentially, give yourself enough time.

Also, to better understand your users on a continual basis, there are some data pathways you should set up to keep information about your users funneling in regularly. This will also make the prep work described above much easier. For example, set up clickstream analytics with a tool *(Google Analytics, Amplitude, Hotjar, etc.)* that allows you to understand what your users are doing with your product. That way, when it comes time to do the prep work for your next design sprint, you already have those metrics ready for analysis. Have an in-app feedback button on your product that allows users the chance to express their attitude toward the site. This will simplify the research process and help set up your design sprint feedback, as well.

In conclusion, a successful design sprint prep empowers the participants to understand the story about your user group, specifically in relation to the problem statement. Use the *"2 Hour Design Sprint"* template in Figma FigJam[13] or another tool of your choice to showcase the story of the user. Provide succinct information to your design sprint participants that you've distilled through your research. Be mindful not to present too much information or present information that is not relevant to the problem statement. Remember, you will only have 20 or so minutes to explain what is known with regard to your users' behaviors and attitudes. Good luck in your learning process!

# PART II: LEARN ABOUT THE TWO HOUR DESIGN SPRINT PROCESS

**CHAPTER 6**

# *STAGE 1 EMPATHIZE WITH CUSTOMERS (30 MINUTES)*

## Intro and Review *(5 minutes)*

- Discuss the two hour design sprint process.

- Set the timer for 3-5 minutes.

Empathy is the core to understanding customer problems. In this first stage, you should spend around 30 minutes in total. The first five minutes are dedicated to a quick review of the agenda and rules, as well as an introduction to Figma FigJam or any collaborative whiteboard tool you plan to use. We will explore whiteboard tool options further in Chapter 12: *"Conduct Your 2 Hour Design Sprint."* You will want to remind each attendee that this is a dedicated and focused two hours and that means turning off devices and committing to engage fully in the session. The two hour design sprint process works so well primarily because of efficiencies manifested during the process. And that requires full collaboration by all participants to achieve success. For example, each participant has the ability to see and absorb problems together on the screen for ideating and reaching agreement on a solution as a group.

## Problem Statement, Goals & Vision *(5 minutes)*

- Agree on the problem statement and goals.

- Set the timer for 3-5 minutes.

The next five minutes are dedicated to reaching agreement on a problem statement and goals for the two hour design sprint. Remember to set a timer. You should already have a constructive draft of the problem statement and goals before starting the design sprint. It is best to have a draft outlined in Figma FigJam, see Figure 6.1, and use this to guide the discussion with the group. Ask whether anyone has edits or additions to either. Problem statements capture the scope of the issues you are tackling in the design sprint and prioritize goals you are seeking to meet as a group.

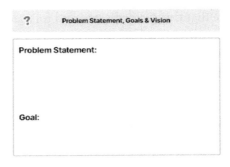

*Figure 6.1*

Key questions to think about as a group when writing the problem statement and goal include:

- Why solve this problem?

- What are the benefits or gaps?

- What is the outcome for the users?

- Who are you solving this problem for?

## Empathize with Customers *(20 minutes)*

- Review current pain points, needs and understandings of users.

- Storyboard and add virtual sticky notes individually.

- Vote as individuals using stamps on top three pain points for end-users.

- Set the timer for 15-20 minutes.

## Timer & Music

Here is a look at the timer available in Figma FigJam *(Figure 6.2)*.

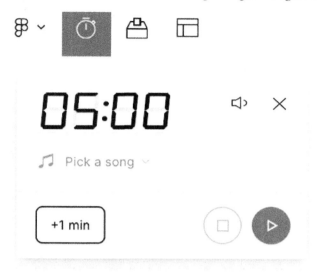

*Figure 6.2*

In addition to the time function, it allows you to play music to keep stakeholders at ease and avoid awkward silence. Before this feature was available, I would often find a workday mix in Spotify[1] to play. So, if you don't plan to use this timer or the music feature, you could certainly look at other options, as well. However, it's important to avoid potential distractions that might take the group off-task. So, I highly recommend using the built-in timer and music feature for the most seamless experience to run an effective two hour design sprint.

## Current Understanding of Customers

The final 20 minutes are focused on empathy and further understanding your customers. As a group, you may discuss the opportunity or problem you are here to solve together. You also may discuss the types of customers that would benefit from a solution and begin to understand real pain points they are experiencing. If using the Figma FigJam[2] template, this exploration of users would be added to the *"Current Understanding of Users"* section. Each stakeholder is encouraged to fill out one or more virtual sticky notes during this section *(Figure 6.3)*. You will want to set the timer for 15-20 minutes and encourage all stakeholders to begin typing what they know about their users. This is divided into two sections, including what works well and what doesn't work well.

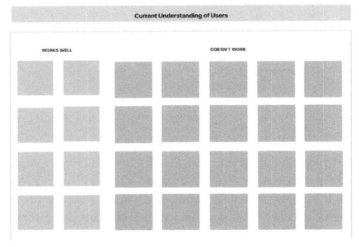

*Figure 6.3*

## What Works Well and What Doesn't Work Well

Let's say you are evaluating the creation of a new mobile app for a dashboard. Currently the dashboard is available via the website for mobile users, but the website is not responsive, and therefore leaves a poor experience for the end user. Users may begin typing what works well and what doesn't work well into the virtual sticky notes. To make the best use of this process, it may be helpful to fill out one or two sticky notes for each area to encourage participation by all stakeholders:

### Works Well:

- Able to search for keywords

- Site keeps my location data so I don't have to reenter

### Doesn't Work Well:

- Unable to click on dashboard

- Not able to filter

- Unable to see half the charts

- Hard to find navigation bar

This exercise of listing what works and what doesn't work well for users allows you to empathize with their experience, including what problems they are encountering and how often.

## Parking Lot

As the moderator, any ideas added to the mix that you feel will not be constructive in the two hour process *(because they are too far outside the scope of the design sprint)* need to be added to the parking lot area of the Figma FigJam board *(Figure 6.4)*. You may visit this parking lot a few times or not at all during the process, there is no hard and fast rule.

*Figure 6.4*

## Importance of Empathy

Empathy is core to the foundation of a design sprint as it allows you to put yourself in the shoes of your customer. While user personas are helpful in this exercise, you do not need one or more user personas to know if a customer is experiencing an issue. As a group you're listing key focus areas that you want to solve.

**CHAPTER 7**

# *STAGE 2 EXPLORE THE PROBLEM (30 MINUTES)*

Now that you have defined your problem statement and user personas, it's time to start exploring the problem further. In Stage 2, *"Explore the Problem"* you will lean into the problem and make any modifications to the problem statement. You're not solutioning in this stage, just working to refine the definition of the problem through an exercise using *"How Might We"*[1] statements.

# How Might We Explanation
## (HMW) (5 minutes)

- Discuss the HMW process with your group.

- Set the timer for 3-5 minutes.

The How Might We *(HMW)* concept was invented in the 1970s by Proctor and Gamble and further popularized by IDEO, according to the Nielsen Norman Group.[2] How Might We's *(HMWs)*, frame a challenge into a question to help generate more creative solutions to solve a problem that has been defined. Here are five tips and examples by the Nielsen Norman Group in generating good HMWs that you can use during this portion of the design sprint.[3]

### #1 Start with the Problems (or Insights) You've Uncovered
- Problem: Users aren't aware of the full product offerings.

- HMW: How might we increase awareness of the full product offerings?

### #2 Avoid Suggesting a Solution in Your HMW Question
- Problem: Users are often unsure about which form to complete when they file their taxes.

- HMW: How might we make users feel confident they are filing their taxes correctly?

### #3 Keep Your HMWs Broad
- Problem: Users often spend a long time checking their submission for mistakes.

- HMW: How might we support users to efficiently draft submissions that they're happy with?

### #4 Focus Your HMWs on the Desired Outcome
- Problem: Users often call us because they're unsure about

the application process.

- HMW: How might we make users feel confident they have all the information they need?

### #5 Phrase Your HMW Questions Positively

- Problem: Users find the return process difficult.

- HMW: How might we make the return process quick and intuitive?

## HMW Exercise *(15 minutes)*

- Fill out your HMW statements.

- Storyboard and have each stakeholder add virtual sticky notes individually.

- Set the timer for 10-15 minutes.

Set a timer for 10-15 minutes and begin filling out your HMW statements in the Stage 2 Explore the Problem section of the Figma FigJam board *(Figure 7.1)*. In addition to the great tips from the Nielsen Norman Group, you will notice in these examples each HMW was framed into a question. Think of ways to turn the problem into an opportunity.

How Might We Exercise (How might we frame the challenge into a question?)

*Figure 7.1*

## Vote on Top Three Problem Explorations *(5 minutes)*

- Vote as individuals using virtual stamps on the top three problem explorations for end-users.

- Discuss top three problem explorations and agree on the final top three.

- Make sure to agree on who the user persona is for each problem exploration.

- Set the timer for 3-5 minutes.

## What Do You Know about the Problem?

In this stage, you are defining what you do know and don't know about the problem. As you learned from John in the Interlude: *"The Importance of Discovery Research Before the Two Hour Design Sprint"* user personas are a research tool to help you better understand your customers. I also shared with you an example of a user persona from my final five day design sprint in Chapter 3: *"Evolution of the Design Sprint."* The persona was called Austin the Analyst. If you're not using personas today or are not very familiar with this concept, you should have all the tools you need to get started in creating your first user personas before the two hour design sprint.

## Virtual Voting on Highest Value Item

Once your timer is up, the next step is voting on the ideas with the highest value as a group. If you have participated in an in-person design sprint, virtual voting replaces physically putting dot stickers or stars on sticky notes. During an in-person design sprint, you are walking around the room trying to read the handwriting of your co-workers and think through what will add the most value for the customer. While I do miss getting in extra steps for the day to tally on my Apple Watch,[4] virtual voting in Figma FigJam is amazing.

## Stamp Feature in Figma FigJam

Each stakeholder gets three votes on the items they feel are of the highest value to solve their customers' problems. FigJam has an array of stamps from which to choose *(Figure 7.2)*, but you're welcome to use your picture or an icon with the initial of your name.

*Figure 7.2*

## Focus on Item with the Most Votes

Once the time is up, you will see which ideas had the most votes. While the image in Figure 7.3 does not include the text examples for the HMWs, the visual will allow you to see how the voting will look once completed. You will be able to identify which ideas you should focus on as a group in Stage 3, *"Ideate Solutions."* If there is a tie between two items, be sure to talk about it as a group to determine which solution would be best to move forward on as a group. For example, some problems may overlap or be outside the scope of the design sprint.

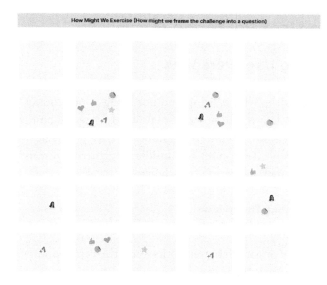

*Figure 7.3*

## Parking Lot

As discussed in Chapter 6 ***"Stage 1 Empathize with Customers,"*** the parking is for any ideas that may be out of scope to complete during the two hour design sprint. Any items that don't get the most votes can be moved to the parking lot for discussion at a later time.

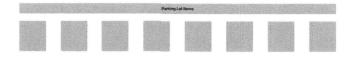

*Figure 7.4*

# Add User Personas *(5 minutes)*

## Creating User Personas

If you are new to creating user personas, you want to start with understanding who is using and not using your product. The amount of data you have access to probably depends on the size of your organization and the number of data points available. Some example data points to consider in gathering research for your customers or personas include:

### Customer Interviews

- Interview at least 5-10 customers for each user role.

- Shadow on-site to better understand their pain points and day-to-day jobs.

- Try to understand and evaluate the problem versus having them tell you.

- Learn about interests, goals, pains, needs and solutions.

### Salesforce[5] or Microsoft CRM[6]

- Identify customer types and roles to determine how many personas you should create.

- Read from comments or themes from support calls or emails.

- Shadow or listen in on calls from customers to have a deeper understanding as to the reason for the call.

### Google Analytics[7] or Amplitude[8]

- If your product is a website or mobile app, and you have analytics data available, look for trends in the data.

### Competitive Research

- Research to see if your competitors have posted any information on their product roles or user personas.

**Medallia⁹ or Qualtrics¹⁰**
* If you have Net Promoter Score *(NPS)* survey data, be sure to look through the comments and find trends.

Once you have gathered this information, you may add it to the user persona section on the FigJam whiteboard as shown in Figure 7.5, if you have not done so already.

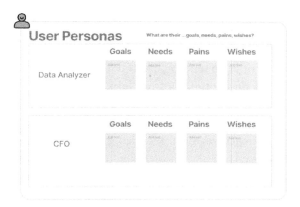

*Figure 7.5*

## ChatGPT¹¹ for User Personas

There has been much chatter in the UX space about using Chat-GPT for UX Research. Moti Sarig,¹² a UX Designer at UniqUI posted about their experience on LinkedIn using ChatGPT to generate Artificial Intelligence *(AI)*-driven user personas to guide the development of a healthcare solution. This post garnered a number of comments and provides an interesting glimpse into this space as we look for ways to automate UX research. When I started writing this book, I had not yet tested ChapGPT due to the waiting list¹³ created to manage demand for the product.

## Before Testing ChatGPT

I do have expertise in building supervised and unsupervised learning models organically and through open APIs[14] for Natural Language Processing *(NLP)*[15] and text analytics[16] solutions. I've also integrated with IBM Watson[17] and Google Translate's Translation API[18]. Based on my experiences, the biggest challenge with ChatGPT is the accuracy of the AI in fine-tuning the algorithms. As it is both supervised and reinforced learning techniques, in order to have the most accurate personas, you would need to constantly send ChatGPT data corrections for any search criteria that was incorrect, also knowing other users could be sending ChatGPT incorrect data, or that ChatGPT is simply pulling from fake or inaccurate websites. At TreviPay, we have more than 20 user personas, so we may very well test ChatGPT and see what we come up with. Based on my experience with the accuracy of AI solutions, I think it could be used as an additional data model in validating use cases to expedite decisions for users, especially for two hour design sprints. However, I do not see it replacing existing UX research or disrupting Nielsen Norman Group's prediction that technology organizations will experience an increase in UX professionals by a factor of 100 by 2050.[19]

## After Testing ChatGPT

I've built and tested many AI tools and technologies with good results,[20] so I dipped my toe into the ChapGPT waters with an open mind. First off, the value ChatGPT brings is its speed and simplicity to conduct research. You start by typing your persona demographics into a browser and the technology generates data immediately to your fingertips. However, tech observers note that ChatGPT presents a threat so evident that it could become a major industry disruption.[21] Like any emerging technology tool, there are pros and cons to consider. The upside is, the output is highly intuitive and creative. The downside is ChatGPT produces text that can have re-used phrases within it, which is plagiarism. This poses an obvious threat to anyone with content housed online and floods the digital space with privacy and security landmines to navigate.

**CHAPTER 8**

# *STAGE 3 IDEATE SOLUTIONS (60 MINUTES)*

S tage 3, *"Ideate Solutions"* is the final stage of the Alpha segment in the two hour design sprint process. It is my favorite stage because this is when all of the brainstorming discussions come together and you get to see how each stakeholder views a solution for the problem. You will notice in the agenda, the majority of the time in a two hour design sprint is dedicated to this stage.

## Explain Sketching Exercise *(5 minutes)*

- Explain sketching exercises for visualizing potential solutions.

- Work individually to explore the problem – free form using paper or Figma FigJam or any tool to draw or convey.

- Set the timer for 3-5 minutes.

Each stakeholder must participate in the sketching exercise. The sketching exercise is exactly how it sounds in that all stakeholders will draw, write, design or show what they believe is the best solution to the top three problem explorations from *Stage 2 Explore the Problem*. While it may be great to have a designer participate as a stakeholder in this exercise, it is not meant to provide high fidelity designs and everyone is an artist.

## Begin Sketching Exercise *(20 minutes)*

- Work individually to explore a solution to the problem using paper, Figma FigJam or any tool to draw or convey your idea.

- Set the timer for 20-25 minutes.

Participating stakeholders will each have their own preference to demonstrate their solution and they can use any tool to do so in the allotted time, as long as they upload it to the sketching area of the whiteboard when the timer is up. I sometimes include a sketch or two of different styles from previous two hour design sprints such as paper sketches, Balsamiq[1] and virtual sticky notes so the group can understand options. We will walk through some example sketches later on in the book. You will likely have a mix of attendees who have participated in five day or two hour design sprints. I prefer paper sketches or Balsamiq. While I enjoy using

Figma[2] and Figma FigJam,[3] some participants find that using online design tools or virtual sticky notes to convey concepts is challenging and prefer to draw on paper.

## How to Make Toast in Three Minutes by Tom Wujec

If you have stakeholders who are really struggling with this exercise, or if design sprints are entirely new to the organization, you may consider walking them through a wildly popular problem-solving tool. It's a teambuilding exercise called *"Draw How to Make Toast."*[4] Tom Wujec is the creator behind this problem-solving exercise and did a famous TedTalk in 2015 called: *"Got a Wicked Problem? First Tell Me How You Make Toast."*[5] If you have never watched this nine minute video, followed by a three minute problem-solving challenge, do yourself a favor. Watch it, and share it with your teams. I've led this exercise with many teams over the years, and it's also taught in schools as a problem-solving tool to foster creativity and innovation in the classroom. During my Master's of Integrated Innovation for Products & Services degree at Carnegie Mellon University, one of my favorite professors Susanna Zlotnikov, who teaches the series on Product Design Innovation,[6] runs this exercise with her students. If you are not ready to commit to a full Master's degree at Carnegie Mellon University, their Integrated Innovation Institute also offers online certificates,[7] including one on Product Design Innovation. It amazes me how many different ways people come up with to make toast during this exercise. Spoiler alert: As shown in the TedTalk and on Wujec's website, participants have just three minutes to draw how to make toast. Wujec's exercise is used in top universities, like Carnegie Mellon's Integrated Innovation Institute, because it teaches a basic problem-solving skill and compels people to think outside the box. In fact, this very exercise I learned years ago is what inspired me to shorten the length of design sprints. I knew a full day of sketching was not needed to be successful in solutioning as a team. If Tom Wujec can teach people to problem solve in three minutes, I can certainly teach people to take a modified approach and solve problems in two hours. And while it may be a longer timeframe, we are talking about solving bigger problems than burning your toast.

## Upload to FigJam *(5 minutes)*

- Stakeholders may upload their finished product to FigJam.

I recommend giving your stakeholders a five minute warning to finish sketching and upload to the FigJam whiteboard. Explain they will paste their solution to the problem exploration in the dedicated sketch exercise space.

*Figure 8.1*

## Presentation *(20 minutes)*

- All attendees get 1-2 minutes to present the value prop of their solution.

- Set the timer for 20 minutes.

As the moderator shows each sketch on the screen in Figma FigJam, have the stakeholder who created it talk about the sketch for 1-2 minutes.

## Vote on Highest Value
## Solution *(5 minutes)*

- Vote as individuals using stamps on top three solutions for end-users.

- Agree on the item with the most votes.

- Set the timer for 5 minutes.

Once the time is up, you will see which ideas received the most votes. If there is a tie between two items, be sure to talk about it as a group to determine which solution would be best to advance. This highest value solution will move forward into the Omega phase, i.e., the two stages outside of the two hour design sprint: prototyping and testing. We will talk about the benefits of moving prototyping and testing stages outside of the two hour design sprint in Chapter 9: *"Stage 4 & 5 Prototype and Test."*

## Workshop Summary &
## Next Steps *(5 minutes)*

- Ask stakeholders if they think the group has the right solution for the problem.

- Summary and next steps.

- Set the timer for 5 minutes.

In the workshop closer, bring up the problem statement and user personas initially discussed. Ask stakeholders if they think the group has come up with a solution for the problem.

### Group Agrees on Solution

If a majority of the group agrees that it is the solution you should bring into prototyping and testing, thank your stakeholders for their time, attendance and creativity and proceed with

Chapter 9: *"Stage 4 & 5 Prototype and Test."* This highest-value solution is what you will bring into the Omega phase to conduct the two stages outside of the two hour design sprint with prototyping and testing to further explore and validate your assumptions.

## Group Disagrees on Solution

If a majority of the group does not agree the solution should advance to prototyping and testing, thank your stakeholders for their time, attendance and creativity. Let them know you will work on researching and redefining the problem statement, and will include them in an additional two hour design sprint.

# Key Differentiator of Two Hour Design Sprints

Choosing whether to move onto prototyping and testing is a key differentiator between a two hour design sprint and a five day design sprint. In a five day design sprint, even if there's disagreement as a group, you still look to prototype and test with users to validate or invalidate your assumptions as a group. Two hour design sprints allow you to make the decision before you invest additional time in prototyping and testing. Keep in mind, you've only spent two hours to get to this conclusion because of the more time-efficient process. If you had not reached a consensus for the solution with a five day design sprint, you would have spent more than 40 hours of your time and stakeholder time, leaving the team feeling incredibly defeated and empty-handed with no solution. Instead, you now have the feedback you need to revise the problem statement and have a constructive two hour design sprint for the next round.

**CHAPTER 9**

# *STAGE 4 & 5 PROTOTYPE AND TEST*

## Prototype and Test After the Two Hour Design Sprint

Another key difference between two hour design sprints and traditional five day design sprints is the recommendation to conduct prototyping and testing outside of the two hour design sprint process. This allows you to control the amount of time you spend on solving a problem for users and to be more certain about the solution when spending valuable time with your designers so that it will be the solution that solves problems for your customers and users.

## Why After the Two Hour Design Sprint?

Two full days for prototyping and testing are allocated on days four and five of a five day design sprint. In the two hour design sprint method, prototyping and testing have been moved outside of the process. They also are condensed to stay more focused on the solution. Recall that in a five day design sprint, you are scheduling testing with users based on the assumption that your prototype is for those user personas. If the users you lined up in advance to test the solution are the right personas, you also are hoping that your solution will be prototype-ready to have them test it and provide valuable enough feedback. Even with a five day design sprint, more design changes and testing are often needed, even after you've already spent the full five days. So, why not spend just two hours and resolve some of the challenges on the front end instead of trying to shoehorn everything into one week.

## Prototyping & Testing Challenges with Five Day Design Sprints

In my experience with five day design sprints, day four of prototyping puts unequal pressure on the designers compared to the rest of the stakeholder team. One night several years ago, a designer and I stayed up until 3 a.m. trying to get a prototype ready for the next day, which ultimately turned our five day design sprint into a six day design sprint. In addition, several of the users we had lined up to attend on day five to test the prototype did not show. So, not only did we not get the feedback we needed, it was also a very expensive meeting and wasted the time of high-value employees who could have been solving other problems for the organization. Squeezing prototyping into a specific timeframe, such as day four of a five day design sprint, could lead to rushed designs and decisions to meet an artificial deadline. It also could lead you to receive feedback and recommendations from the wrong user persona if clients do a last-minute swap for testing on day five. In addition to users not showing up for scheduled testing when you have a room full of stakeholders eager to capture their feedback, you might only be solving for one persona and would still need to conduct additional prototyping and testing outside of the five day design sprint.

Moving prototyping and testing outside of the two hour design sprint takes arbitrary pressure out of the equation and adds value to the process. It gives the group more time to solidify the design and practice better decision-making to come up with the best elements for your users to test. It also makes common sense to have ample time to schedule the right user personas to test the solution.

## Schedule for Prototyping after the Two Hour Design Sprint

### Prototype *(2-4 hours)*

- High-fidelity designs.

- Build prototype.

Bear in mind that two hour design sprints are recommended for small or medium-sized problems. In my experience, high fidelity designs or prototypes can be completed in four hours and ready for testing, however, it will be dependent on your design team's familiarity with the concept. Now, if you are using two hour design sprints to solve a larger or more complex problem, you should expect this time to increase.

### Who Should Work on the Prototype?

I have worked with large, complex technology organizations that employ robust design and UX teams in the double digits, as well as firms with no designers or UX team members at all. Two hour design sprints are appealing to organizations that need to move at a rapid pace, including startups or firms that may not have their entire tech team built out. I have worked in a number of product manager roles in my career where I was also the designer creating concepts on paper, based on user feedback, then moving on to higher fidelity concepts in Balsamiq,[1] Sketch[2] and InVision.[3] This was of course before Figma[4] existed. I've also had to create prototypes in my time as a project manager and ScrumMaster. My philosophy is you step in when you need to. The person that should own the prototype is sometimes the person who is available to create the prototype. This again, is one of the challenges of rolling out a cookie cutter process at companies that do not have the breadth of resources like Google. However, in an ideal scenario, you would have your UX designer create high-fidelity design and prototypes for testing. I have been incredibly spoiled the last several years and work with and manage a stellar group of designers. I kid you not, they can knock out a high fidelity design and prototype in an hour if I need them too, they are so talented. If you don't have access to a deep designer bench, I would lean on your UX researcher or product manager to get the prototype created. Most product managers are accustomed to filling this gap in their roles already. In fact, what attracted me to the world of product management is the versatility in the role from selling, meeting with customers, designing, strategizing and building competitive roadmaps. If you do not have a product manager, designer or UX researcher or you're a lean team at a small startup with a handful of roles, you could look to hire this out using a third party design firm like Blink UX[5], YML[6] or BullPen[7] or contract designers from sites like Dribble,[8] 99Designs[9] or Fiverr.[10]

If none of these options is in your budget, you will need to delegate this task to someone on your team to learn. There are many free trainings available online or paid courses on sites like Udemy.[11] I have a training session on Udemy specifically created for two hour design sprints.[12] You can pick up the skills needed to create higher fidelity designs and prototypes in no time. Ultimately, the most important factor to consider in the design is conveying your story or solution to the client so that they can provide the proper feedback to achieve the best solution to the problem.

## Physical Prototypes

Physical prototypes usually take more time, regardless if it's a two hour design sprint or five day design sprint simply because you might be sending designs off to a manufacturer to get samples back to put in front of your users for testing. Two hour design sprints cater very well to physical products because it would be virtually impossible for many physical products to be ready for testing on day five of a five day design sprint. Two hour design sprints allow you to finalize designs sooner and get prototypes back faster. Getting prototypes back faster enables the team to evaluate the solution before getting it in front of users.

# Schedule for Testing after the Two Hour Design Sprint

## Testing *(2-4 hours)*

- Schedule testing with 5-7 users per persona.

- Review testing feedback as a group.

- Set the timer for 5 minutes.

Once the prototype is ready, testing is the final step in your process to learn whether the solution you came up with as a team is solving problems for your users. This step will help you decide whether you should move forward with implementing the solution, or go back to the drawing board.

## Who Should Be Testing the Prototype?

You want to test users that meet the profile of the user personas you created during the two hour design sprint. This is a critical step in the process to make sure you are getting in front of users who will be using your product. The number of screens you are testing will determine the length of time needed for the session. Other considerations to take into account include what the users will be testing, such as no designs/concept only, high fidelity designs, prototype, or a clickable prototype for the users to walk through on their own or through user scenarios.

In each of these situations, I like to have around 5-7 users and prepare a set of 10-15 questions that allows me to understand their role and day-to-day interaction with the potential solution. This allows me to gain a deeper understanding about the problems they are experiencing before showing them any prototypes. In other words, I don't want to lead with the design as the solution, as it very well might not be the solution. Plan to dedicate 30 minutes for each interview, keep in mind the prototype is the hypothesis that you are testing.

## No Designs, Concepts Only User Testing

In this scenario, you may have a design or prototype ready, or you may not. Whichever the case, you are not 100% confident in the solution. When testing users with no designs and with concepts only, you are completely driven by question-led scenarios and hypotheticals.

## High Fidelity Designs User Testing

When testing a high fidelity design you are showing your users the design and asking question-led scenarios to get their opinion on screens or workflows you have created in high fidelity. This may be one or more screens depending on the problem you were solving as an organization.

## Prototype User Testing

Prototype user testing for the software world is usually done in Figma or InVision in which you are creating a series of screens to create a clickable prototype. To the users, the screens are sometimes so real that they look like a live environment. In the physical product world, this would be a physical prototype that would allow your users to see a physical prototype.

## User-Led Clickable Prototype Testing

User-led clickable prototype testing is where you let the users click where they think they should be clicking, instead of where you think they should be clicking. This could be a prototype in Figma or InVision, or it could be a smoke and mirrors demo environment if your team is equipped with engineers who are able to quickly implement a mock solution in a beta environment.

## User Scenario-Driven Clickable Prototype Testing

User scenario-driven clickable prototype testing is where you type up a scenario for your users to follow and see whether they are able to complete the steps. This is actually my preferred method – if a prototype is ready. I liked to record the user's screen to assess how the tester navigates the features and whether the user is able to find a button or click on certain areas of the page. You could also utilize A/B Testing scenarios where you have different groups test different prototypes. If you are not familiar with A/B Testing, Harvard Business Review put out a great article a few years back on its benefits.[13]

## What if I don't have any Users to Test?

If you have a user base already, but just not one for the persona you are designing for, you will look to closely map which users from your existing products match the profile for the product you are testing. If you are a startup or an organization that has no users to tap, there are many great options such as UserTesting,[14] UsabilityHub,[15] UserInterviews,[16] or Maze.[17] You tell them about the types of users that you want to test your prototype, and they will line them up for you to test concepts, prototypes, and designs. Note they also are available to run the sessions for you on your behalf as a representative of your company.

## The Importance of Customer Feedback

Whether you are conducting a two hour design sprint or a traditional design sprint, getting feedback from your users is the most valuable tool you can have in your tool box before you release a new product, feature or solution to market. Design sprints are one avenue in getting quicker feedback from your clients and users to accelerate the process. During the Interlude, John talked about the importance of research, especially before conducting a two hour design sprint that also applies to traditional design sprints. Some additional ways of getting customer feedback for your products and solutions include in-person site visits, virtual shadowing, customer interviews, focus groups, A/B usability testing, behavioral analytics, and CX surveys.

# PART III: PUT INTO PRACTICE THE CONCEPT OF TWO HOUR DESIGN SPRINTS

CHAPTER 10

# *ADVANTAGES OF USING TWO HOUR DESIGN SPRINTS*

## Time Savings - It's Only Two Hours

The biggest advantage of two hour design sprints is time savings. Instead of devoting five full days exploring a problem, your organization can boil that down to two hours. It is also much easier to gather 10-50 key stakeholders for two hours rather than 40 hours. Speaking from years of experience, I have not participated in or conducted a single five day design sprint in which every single stakeholder was able to stay and participate during the entire five day commitment. If you don't have the right stakeholder group's attention for the full design sprint, you're not going to solve the right problem or come up with the right solution. More likely than not, you will spend time on the wrong problems if you're missing input from key stakeholders.

## Global Collaboration - Everyone Can Be 100% Remote

For larger organizations, it can be challenging to book a room for an in-person design sprint for five full days. If you are an organization with offices located all over the globe, running a five day, in-person design sprint with stakeholders from Australia, U.S. and the UK will add substantial expenses to fly in key team members for the big event. The two hour design sprint process better accommodates the budget and schedules for key stakeholders who work halfway around the world. So, while your stakeholders in Australia may be one day ahead of others in the design sprint, clocking in bright and early at 7 a.m. local time on a Thursday, your Washington D.C. team members would still be able to join the collaboration at 3 p.m. local time on a Wednesday. The best part is, everyone is able to make the time commitment for the entire two hour design sprint.

## Less Setup Time - Replace Post-its with Virtual Sticky Notes

One item that is often overlooked when considering five day design sprints is the amount of time that goes into setting up the room before the start of each day, as well as preparation for the next day. Without exception, every five day design sprint that I ran was time-consuming and exhausting, even before the day got started. I'd be in the room the night before, taping pieces of large white paper to the walls, organizing boxes of Post-it notes, markers and stickers. Once you finish each day, you are then trying to organize concepts so that everyone is up-to-speed in the morning to save time explaining where you left off the day before. Conducting *"2 Hour Design Sprints"* eliminates much of this setup with the whiteboard collaborative tools that can be used for remote or in-person design sprints.

The setup in Figma FigJam is minimal when using the *"2 Hour Design Sprints"* template posted on the FigJam community. What's even better, you simply email the Figma FigJam design sprint link to your team after your meeting. With a five day design sprint, it takes a few days to gather and analyze your outcomes and type it up to send to the group. What's more, you're left with a ton of paper, Post-it notes and markers at your desk that you hang on to for weeks, debating whether to throw it away or keep it in case you missed something. I will say the one thing I do miss about the setup is bringing in specialty coffee or breakfasts for the team. However, it's still possible to thank attendees on your stakeholder team for their participation by having coffee and treats delivered to their doors with the many online ordering tools and mobile ordering apps available at your fingertips. I really love local coffee shops, but it's also very convenient that Starbucks now delivers treats via DoorDash or UberEats[1].

## Anyone on the Team Can Be a Moderator - No Third Parties

One of the key differences between a five day and two hour design sprint is that anyone on the team can be a moderator for a two hour design sprint. Over the years this mindset has really changed. Many of the consulting firms I previously worked with recommended only non-subject matter experts should serve as the moderator. What's more, they believed that a third party vendor should facilitate the five day design sprint and be the one to make recommendations, not the team of field experts participating in the design sprint. Let me remind you, it gets very expensive to bring in a third party to run a design sprint. The contract ranges anywhere from $10,000 to $100,000 depending on the range of services you need. For example, third party vendors can provide facilitating, training and help execute prototypes and testing. In addition to the added costs, the biggest challenge I experienced using outside firms was the extra time spent educating the trainer about your business, your products, your problems and explaining the subject matter for which the design sprint is needed. This was highly inefficient and a complete waste of time in my opinion. In fact, the five day design sprint can be reduced to a three day timeline if you use a subject matter expert *(SME).* I have led many three day design sprints before moving to two hours by cutting out the time that would have been spent getting an outside moderator up to speed. It will not be a surprise for you to hear me reiterate this is a huge reason why two hour design sprints are so successful. SMEs not only make great moderators, they make better moderators than an outside third party facilitator. Based on my experience, I highly recommend using a SME as your moderator. This jump starts the design sprint process. Right out of the gate, the SME can lead the team to success by getting all the stakeholders to empathize with the problem at hand and cohesively solution together. Anyone on the team can be a moderator, but it should be someone who already has a grasp of the subject matter or feature that's being talked about. It can be a team member from product, UX, design, engineering, scrum coach or anyone from any part of the organization who is familiar with the business. As a moderator, you are also a key contributor to the discussion. So, you get to wear two hats during this process. That adds up to twice the fun in less time.

## Collaborative Whiteboard Tools for Remote Collaboration

In Chapter 4: *"History of UX,"* we examined a key element for the success of implementing two hour design sprints is the digital tools now available to support remote collaboration, including InVision Freehand, Miro and Figma FigJam. I have used all three whiteboard tools for two hour design sprints, but I am a big fan of Figma FigJam. I have been using the beta version of its collaborative whiteboard since 2021 and also migrated most of my teams over from Invision FreeHand. I recommend Figma for design and prototyping and Figma FigJam for two hour design sprints. Many workshop attendees mention they use Mural and enjoy it as well. See Figure 10.1 to familiarize yourself with the two hour design sprint template in Figma FigJam. If you search for **"2 Hour Design Sprints"** by Teresa Cain in the FigJam community site,[2] you can find this board for reference. If you prefer to use another collaborative tool besides Figma FigJam, you may easily recreate this board *(see Figure 10.1)*. Figma FigJam, InVision FreeHand and Miro all have free accounts for using three projects or less. Figma FigJam has unlimited collaborators, Invision Freehand has up to 100 active collaborators, and Miro has no collaborator option for their free account at the time of publication.

*Figure 10.1*

# Documentation and Design in One Location

No matter the tool you choose to run your two hour design

sprint, the greatest advantage is the ability to have documentation and design in one place. Whether it's the virtual sticky notes used for understanding customers, *"How Might We's"* *(HMWs)* or brainstorming solutions through the sketch exercise, all the content you are working on together as a group is right in front of you. This allows participants to make key decisions at a thorough but faster pace due to the efficiencies created in using these tools. You no longer have to walk around the room trying to read handwriting from your teammates. Everything you need to interact and make decisions within the two hour design sprint is right in front of you. This concept of using a collaborative whiteboard tool runs counter to the traditional five day design sprint rules of limiting devices for engagement. The irony is that in five day design sprints, stakeholders may not have their devices in the room. However, if they leave to take a call or email on their device, they are disengaging with the design sprint and adding a distraction that could impact the solution the team comes up with together.

With the two hour design sprint process, you are committing as a team to solving your problem in two hours and having full team engagement during the process. I have not had to do this for two hour design sprints, but if you really wanted to put metrics around engagement to retain focus, you could use a tool like Webex[3] to track participant attention. Zoom previously offered an attendee attention tracking feature but removed it in 2020 citing its commitment to security and privacy of customers.[4] The intent of using a collaborative tool is that you are able to see the engagement from all stakeholders working in the FigJam file together at once. I will be curious to see whether Figma adds any tracking in the future to FigJam if the Adobe acquisition goes through, currently it has a feature to view and export activity logs.[5] Ultimately though, I've noticed the visual collaboration tool used in a two hour design sprint achieves much higher engagement, better focus and input from stakeholders who are actively participating in the solution. This allows the organization to get their clients a solution more efficiently and ultimately build revenue faster.

## Sketch Using any Tool

Another great advantage with digital tools is it expands more effective collaboration opportunities. You are not limited to paper sketches! Attendees can choose any online tool they would like to sketch their idea for a solution. Even for those who still enjoy paper sketching, they can easily upload their sketch to Figma FigJam. In a traditional design sprint, participants sketch solutions on paper. This may come with limitations on time and creativity for some who prefer to use tools meant for low fidelity sketching outside of Figma or Figma FigJam such as Balsamiq,[6] quick workflows using Lucidchart[7] or rapid designs using Canva.[8] Digital tools also save so much time by eliminating the need to walk around the room looking at different designs and deciphering handwriting styles. Collaborative tools like Figma FigJam have all the designs from stakeholders right in front of the participants. Any questions about the designs can be added in a comment on the design or by asking questions when the solution is presented to the group.

## Virtual Voting on High Value Features

Figma FigJam makes voting on highest-value features easy! In Chapter 7: *"Stage 2 Explore the Problem,"* we talked about virtual voting in Figma FigJam and how it replaces physically putting dot stickers or stars on virtual sticky notes as one would during a traditional five day design sprint. By using the stamp feature in Figma FigJam stakeholders can vote seamlessly on their top three items. It takes away the hectic scenario where a roomful of participants are rushing around the space. They no longer have to wander around the room like they are at an art gallery, trying to remember the name of the artist and meaning behind the drawing. With Figma FigJam, virtual voting is online and keeps everything in one place. So, you're able to absorb the information in real time and assign your top vote on the best solution to help solve problems for your customers. This process improves engagement with stakeholders and with less time commitment than traditional methods because every attendee is along for the full journey of the two hour design sprint.

## Multiple Design Sprints in a Week - Implement Solutions Faster for Your Clients

Another key advantage of the two hour design sprint is the ability to conduct multiple design sprints in a week or month. The five day design sprint method boxes in your organization for an entire work week, and potentially precludes your team from bringing your solution into the next agile sprint. With two hour design sprints, you could start your two hour design sprint process on a Monday and by Friday be ready to have your engineering team work on the feature. That's not really feasible with five day design sprints, and not only because of the amount of time dedicated to the process. Typically, you're solving very large, complex problems and may not be ready to pull the solution into the sprint. From my experience, your engineering leads and architects may want to dive further into the solution before committing to the design. With two hour designs prints, you're able to get multiple designs out faster and in front of clients for their feedback. You are also able to get those features released more quickly, whether you have a one-, two-, three- or four-week agile sprint or if using the Kanban method. You may even agree as a team that users don't find the priority as high as a priority as expected, so you might end up putting the feature on your backlog or long-term roadmap. The goal of the two hour design sprint is to eliminate holes in your design faster, instead of throwing away concepts after spending five days on it. Ultimately, you can implement faster solutions for your clients. Even if you learn from users that what your team came up with after the two hour design sprint is not the best solution, you can plan a second two hour design sprint to come up with a better solution. Then you haven't lost five days of productivity on a solution that doesn't fit and you're making better use of time with more effective results and less risk.

**CHAPTER 11**

# *ADDITIONAL PREP FOR A SUCCESSFUL TWO HOUR DESIGN SPRINT*

## Create Stakeholder List

When creating your stakeholder list, take into account which team members need to attend to help solve the problem, as well as individuals needed to get their buy-in for the final solution. Make sure to create a diverse list of attendees from across the organization, including stakeholders who interact with your customers or have deep knowledge of their problems. I recommend inviting no more than 20 attendees to the two hour design sprint for best collaboration and focus. I have run two hour design sprints with more than 50 people participating. Although it was productive, not all attendees participated with meaningful engagement. Having a maximum number of 20 participants will allow you to track engagement and moderate interaction with the group, such as to call on individual stakeholders when it's their time to present their sketch or check in with individuals who haven't voted for any of the exercises, such as the HMWs. Make sure to include attendees from different areas of the business, such as:

- 1 Moderator *(Product, UX, Design, Lead or SME)*
- 1 Product Manager
- 1 UX Researcher
- 1 Product Owner
- 1 Designer
- 1 Developer
- 1 QA Analyst
- 1 Technical Architect
- 1 Engineering Lead
- 1 Customer Experience/Support Rep
- 1 Account Manager
- 1 Marketing Manager
- 1 Data Analyst
- 1 Industry Sales Rep
- 1 Partnerships Manager

# Review Figma FigJam Whiteboard

## Finalize Agenda and Use Timer

We discussed the example agenda *(Figure 11.1)* and use of the Figma FigJam timer *(Figure 11.2)* for a two hour design sprint in Chapter 5: *"Impact of Remote Work on Design Sprints."*

**Agenda**

**Intro and Review (5 minutes)**
- Discuss the 2 hour design sprint process.

**Empathize with Customers (25 minutes)**
- Review current pain points, needs and observations of users.
- Storyboard and add to sticky notes individually.
- Vote as individuals using stamps on top three pain points for end-users.

**Explore the Problem (30 minutes)**
- "How might we?" exercise - frame a challenge into a question. How might we solve a problem that has been defined?
- Storyboard and add to sticky notes individually.
- Vote as individuals using stamps on top three problem explorations for end-users.

**Ideate Solutions (30 minutes)**
- Sketching exercise for visualizing potential solution.
- Work individually to explore the problem – free form using paper or Figma or any tool to draw or convey.

**Presentation (20 minutes)**
- All attendees gets 1-2 minutes to present the value prop of their sketch and solution to the problem.

**Group Voting of Ideate Solutions (5 minutes)**
- Vote as individuals using stamps on top three solutions for end-users.

**Workshop Summary & Next Steps (5 minutes)**
- We will take a few minutes to talk about the top two designs and opportunity to move forward as a group with prototyping and testing with customers.

*Figure 11.1*

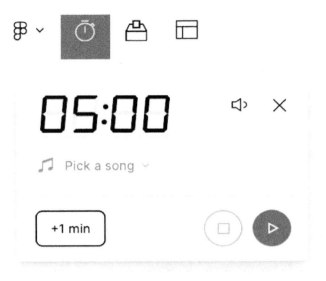

*Figure 11.2*

In preparing for your first design sprint, make sure your Figma FigJam board is ready to go before starting so that the full two hours are used as efficiently as possible. Familiarize yourself with the agenda and timer in Figma FigJam to be able to prompt and introduce topics to the group. As you conduct more design sprints, it will become easier to moderate and keep the pace flowing. The key to effectively moderating design sprints is staying on track through each stage. Be diligent about using the timer in Figma FigJam to stay on schedule. If you are conducting two hour design sprints often, it becomes second nature to guide the agenda and keep participants on track and on time.

## Utilize Parking Lot

If running a two hour design sprint with new stakeholder groups each time, keep in mind that while the experience is familiar for you, it isn't for new participants. So, you will need to guide them through each section and remind them to stay on task. This could mean adding more topics to your parking lot *(Figure 11.3)* to stay focused on the problem you are trying to solve as a stakeholder group.

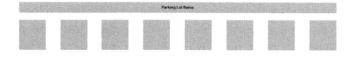

*Figure 11.3*

## Practice Run

Speaking from experience, I advise moderators to carve out time for a mock run-through before gathering the stakeholders for the design sprint. Practice how you plan to introduce the topic and go over the agenda. This is much like running through a presentation before you deliver on the big stage, except you don't need an audience. For example, I like to think about what I will say to stakeholders to bring cohesion to the group for their next two hours together. As I run through each section beforehand, I make sure to watch the time to have a better grasp of transitions and the timetable. If you are not sure how to start off your design sprint or how to conduct one, we will cover this in Chapter 12: *"Conduct Your Two Hour Design Sprint."* Here, I will walk through a mock design sprint in more detail. In addition, check out my training course on Udemy – *"2 Hour Design Sprints: Learn how to solve problems and design products in just 2 hours vs. 5 days using Figma FigJam"*[1] for an online tutorial for using the template in Figma FigJam.

## Design Sprint Rules

Be ready for the unexpected. Bringing together a team of stakeholders for the first time could trigger a trove of topics that may catch the moderator off guard. When introducing the agenda, nip extraneous topics in the bud and remind the group about the specific goals for this two hour design sprint. Agree as a team to focus on the opportunity at hand, not other problems, and ask participants for their undivided attention for the full two hours. Specifically, that means interacting and engaging with one another to come up with the right solution together as a stakeholder team.

## Send Figma FigJam Link to Participants

You may choose to send the Figma FigJam link of your whiteboard before meeting with participants for the design sprint. Alternatively, you may share it when introducing the agenda at the meeting. Sharing the link beforehand allows users to become familiar with the board so they can hit the ground running. However, particularly for those who previously have not participated in a design sprint, the downside is that it may prompt excess questions that would be answered at the start of the session. The upside to sharing the link simultaneously when introducing the agenda is that it doesn't take any advance setup time for the user to be a collaborator. However, should a participant encounter an issue for any reason and require assistance, it would interfere with the introduction and mess with the time table of the two hour design sprint. As Figma FigJam allows for unlimited collaborators, anyone with the link is able to join the collaborative whiteboard. Keep in mind if using any security features such as password protection, be sure to securely share the password with the participants so they are able to gain access.

## Virtual or In-Person

While two hour design sprints helped organizations continue

to collaborate and solve problems as a remote workforce during COVID-19 shutdowns, a majority of the efficiencies can be credited to digital collaborative tools like Figma FigJam. While most of the two hour design sprints I have conducted have been remote, in 2022 I started to implement this process in-person with my team at TreviPay with great success. Like many organizations, the COVID-19 pandemic changed our office policies, originally opening the door for a 100% remote workforce. Now, in a hybrid environment employees may choose to stay remote or come into the office. In addition to having hybrid product management, UX and design teams, we have team members working across the globe. The two hour design sprint process allows for seamless collaboration among team members and enables stakeholders to participate either in-person or remote during the same meeting using Figma FigJam and video conference tools such as Zoom,[2] Microsoft Teams,[3] or Google Meet Video Conferencing.[4] I use all three regularly. Although Zoom does have a fee for meetings beyond 40 minutes, I prefer Zoom for the experience with users and ability to conduct breakout rooms. You also could use any video conferencing software of your choice.

**CHAPTER 12**

# CONDUCT YOUR TWO HOUR DESIGN SPRINT

Good news! You have all the tools you need to conduct a successful two hour design sprint! Now, choose a problem your organization is looking to solve, create your attendee list and agenda, and schedule your two hour design sprint.

## Mock Design Sprint

In this section we will walk through an example of a completed design sprint using the two hour design sprint Figma FigJam template.

## Two Hour Design Sprint Template on Figma FigJam

Search for *"2 Hour Design Sprints"* by Teresa Cain in the Figma FigJam Community.[1] Click on *"Get a Copy"* to duplicate the template for your personal use and begin to fill out the template. You may also walk through a live version of the mock design sprint in my Udemy Course *"2 Hour Design Sprints: Learn how to solve problems and design products in just 2 hours vs. 5 days using Figma FigJam."*[2]

*Figure 12.1*

## Agenda

The pre-filled agenda in Figure 12.2 carves out 120 minutes for the two hour design sprint. Again this process is a recommendation on a modified approach to a traditional design sprint, so you may adjust this agenda as needed to suit the goals and needs of your organization.

---

**Agenda**

**Intro and Review (5 minutes)**
- Discuss the 2 hour design sprint process.

**Empathize with Customers (25 minutes)**
- Review current pain points, needs and observations of users.
- Storyboard and add to sticky notes individually.
- Vote as individuals using stamps on top three pain points for end-users.

**Explore the Problem (30 minutes)**
- "How might we?" exercise - frame a challenge into a question.
How might we solve a problem that has been defined?
- Storyboard and add to sticky notes individually.
- Vote as individuals using stamps on top three problem explorations for end-users.

**Ideate Solutions (30 minutes)**
- Sketching exercise for visualizing potential solution.
- Work individually to explore the problem – free form using paper or Figma or any tool to draw or convey.

**Presentation (20 minutes)**
- All attendees gets 1-2 minutes to present the value prop of their sketch and solution to the problem.

**Group Voting of Ideate Solutions (5 minutes)**
- Vote as individuals using stamps on top three solutions for end-users.

**Workshop Summary & Next Steps (5 minutes)**
- We will take a few minutes to talk about the top two designs and opportunity to move forward as a group with prototyping and testing with customers.

*Figure 12.2*

## Problem Statement & Goals

I recommend the moderator develop a problem statement and goal before starting the two hour design sprint *(see Figure 12.3)*. This prep step will provide strategic guidance to the group to define the problem the team is looking to solve together during the session. This problem statement becomes a stepping stone for team members to modify as a group and make adjustments to the problem statement, goals and vision together.

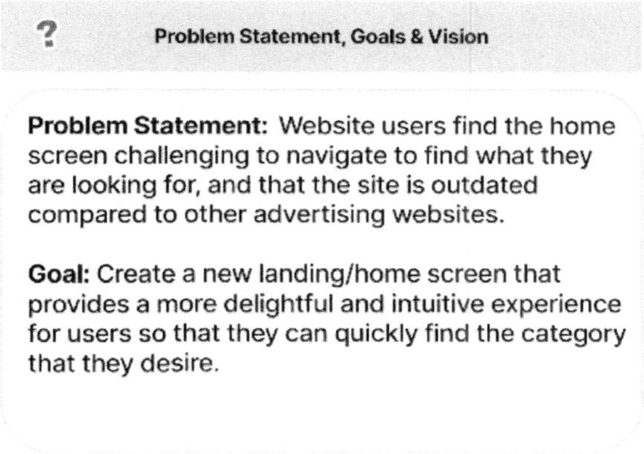

**?**  **Problem Statement, Goals & Vision**

**Problem Statement:** Website users find the home screen challenging to navigate to find what they are looking for, and that the site is outdated compared to other advertising websites.

**Goal:** Create a new landing/home screen that provides a more delightful and intuitive experience for users so that they can quickly find the category that they desire.

*Figure 12.3*

## User Personas

I recommend creating one or two personas for whom you are problem-solving *(see Figure 12.4)*. Fill out their goals, needs, pains, and wishes using the space allotted. If time allows, it would be best to fill these out in advance. Taking this step will help the group discuss and agree on the personas as they relate to the problem statement. Adjust as needed.

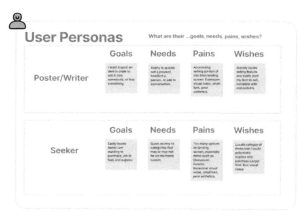

*Figure 12.4*

## Parking Lot

Don't skip this step. Any item or concept that is brought up during the design sprint belongs in the parking lot. As you stay focused on the problem at hand during the two hours, be sure to add any idea, problem, persona or experience that falls outside of that construct to the parking lot. At the conclusion of the two hour design sprint, you have actionable items ready to be addressed in a separate meeting or follow-up design sprint *(see Figure 12.5)*.

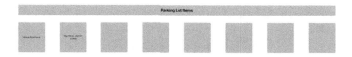

*Figure 12.5*

## Stage 1: Empathize with Customers

Encourage each participant to fill out at least one virtual sticky note for *"Works Well"* and *"Doesn't Work Well."* Before voting begins, I like to combine common themes together for consideration during voting. I make this a group activity and encourage all participants to join in this exercise with a 1-2 minute timer. Once that is done, we vote as a group. By involving participants in this process, it allows each individual to read and understand what each stakeholder thinks is working well and what is not working well. Having the big picture helps better inform their votes. Depending on the number of participants and number of themes, you may stick with three votes per participant. Feel free to make adjustments, but I would not recommend having less than two or more than five votes *(see Figure 12.6)*.

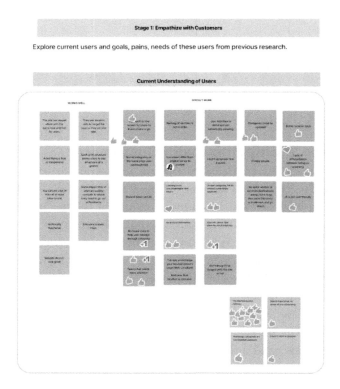

*Figure 12.6*

## Stage 2: Explore the Problem

Encourage each participant to fill out at least one virtual sticky note for the *"How Might We"* exercise. Before voting begins, I like to combine common themes together for consideration during voting. I make this a group activity and encourage all participants to join in this exercise with a 1-2 minute timer. Once that is done, we vote as a group. Depending on the number of participants and number of themes, you may stick with three votes per participant. Feel free to make adjustments, but I would not recommend having less than two or more than five votes *(see Figure 12.7)*.

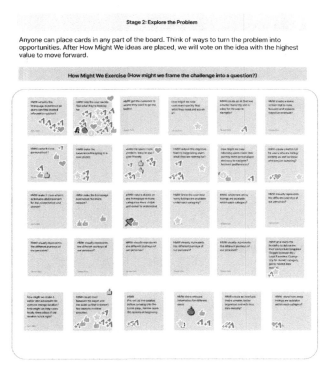

*Figure 12.7*

## Stage 3: Ideate Solutions

In this final stage of ideating solutions, all participants must create a potential solution by either using sketches on paper they can upload, or placing sticky notes on the FigJam board or any other preferred tool. Have participants load their sketches to the Stage 3 *"Ideate Solutions"* board, and be sure to include yours as well. Participants should present their solutions for 1-2 minutes to the group before voting. Try to stick to a minimum of two votes and maximum of three votes per participant. This helps to narrow the best solutions to the problem during the design sprint and provides the roadmap for prototyping and testing with users *(see Figure 12.8)*.

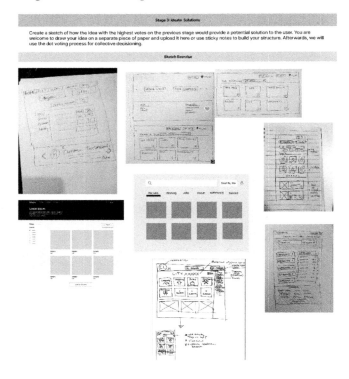

*Figure 12.8*

**CHAPTER 13**

# *FINAL*
# *RECOMMENDATIONS*

## The Decider Role in Two Hour Design Sprints

One question I often get asked during training sessions or conferences, including from Ruben Betancourt from Tango.io., who shares one of the success stories in Chapter 14: *"2 Hour Design Sprint Success Stories"* is this: *"Who is the decider?"* According to the *"Sprint Book"*[1] by Jake Knapp and the team at GV Ventures, the CEO is typically the decider in smaller organizations. In larger organizations, it may be another leader who has authority to make decisions. In this two hour design sprint process, YOU are the decider! You make the recommendations about solutions the team should move forward with after voting and before heading into the prototyping and testing stage. By taking ownership of the two hour design sprint process, you have the authority to make the recommendation to all stakeholders, including to your CEO. After the two hours brainstorming as a team, you will have the stakeholders backing up the path forward and the data to support the solution. Remember, you created the participant list and included key stakeholders to have buy-in for the end product.

## Selling Two Hour Design Sprints to Your Organization

If you have had a hard time selling design thinking or design sprint processes to the top decision makers at your organization, keep in mind the best selling points for conducting a two hour design sprint. It is arguably risk-free and delivers bang for the buck. The process takes less than a day to complete and truly pays it forward. Two hour design sprints will prove the value and merits of UX research and will underscore that making these investments will solve more problems more effectively and efficiently for your organization.

## The Importance of Stakeholder Buy-In

The great news about getting stakeholder buy-in is that you are already one step ahead of the game. Remember, you included key stakeholders in the design sprint process to get their valuable feedback and support. Now you can leverage those relationships to help get buy-in on the final concept when meeting with other key decision-makers. If you are new to the concept of stakeholder feedback or need some new ways to creatively get buy-in from decision-makers at your organization, I recommend keeping your eye on a title coming out soon *"Aligned: Stakeholder Management for Product Leaders"* by O'Reilly Media.[2] One of the authors, Melissa Appel, is a Carnegie Mellon University and Wayfair alum with more than 20 years of product management experience. I asked Melissa about her recommendations for stakeholder feedback as it related to the two hour design sprint process, she said, *"In business, most results can not be achieved in a vacuum. Bringing your key stakeholders along with you on the end-to-end journey for your product allows you to get feedback along the way and not just at the very end. It also makes your stakeholders feel included and consulted, which gives them a sense of ownership at your side."* I couldn't agree more with Melissa on how critical it is to bring your stakeholders along for the whole journey and two hour design sprints allow you to earn their buy-in much earlier in the process.

## Design Sprint to Backlog

So what happens after prototyping and testing? Design sprints are an agile approach and once you have validated your prototype with users, you have a design and concept to begin creating user stories and functional requirements. The size of the design team and SDLC *(software development lifecycle)* that you have at your organization will dictate how quickly you can begin working on user stories. I have brought design sprint concepts in immediately after user validation, however additional iterations may be required pending the skill and comfort level of your teams. As you work with your engineers and designers, much of this will likely depend on whether your concept is entirely new or adding additional functionality to existing screens. Additional meetings with members of your development team may be required as well, depending on their skill level and familiarity with the concept. If you are running agile processes like many technology organizations these days and as referenced in Chapter 3: *"Evolution of the Design Sprint,"* I recommend creating user stories in your backlog and start the grooming[3] process as soon as you finish testing with your users. Some great tools I recommend and use for that process include, DevStride[4], JIRA[5] or TRELLO.[6]

CHAPTER 14

# *TWO HOUR DESIGN SPRINT SUCCESS STORIES*

## Collin Williamson, Senior UX Designer, TreviPay

*In previous roles, I had familiarity with the week-long design sprint method. I helped lead sprints and participate in many, as well. Design sprints felt like a huge undertaking for our team. Each one would build up to be this large event within the company since they required so many hands on deck to make it successful. Sprints were scheduled months in advance and required work from many professionals across all departments within the company.*

*Gathering participants was difficult as few had the time to devote an entire work week for a five day design sprint. There was a lot of pressure to produce an outcome at the end of the week. We couldn't afford not to deliver a solution when the sprint wrapped up due to the investment of time and effort we had given throughout the week.*

*Because of these variables, we rarely ran design sprints and our users suffered because of it. Many features or requests were created in a vacuum simply because there wasn't enough time to conduct five day sprints. I was skeptical when I was introduced to the two hour design sprint concept. I didn't think it was possible to get thoughtful and valuable ideas within such a short amount of time. To the contrary, the two hour design sprint removed a lot of pressure from the participants and facilitators and allowed creativity and problem solving to flow. Two hour design sprints are short enough to easily schedule with users and participants and produce valuable insights and solutions for the time required to run them.*

*My first two hour design sprint revolved around developing a requested feature from our customers and championed by our account management team. This feature wasn't overly exhaustive to put in place, but it lacked any kind of direction on what the next step would be. We also struggled to identify what the key user pain points were, so building a solution was often vague and success was difficult to define.*

*The desired feature didn't feel like it deserved a week-long design sprint dedicated to problem-solving for it. So, it was the perfect candidate for a smaller, quicker sprint. Armed with the limited knowledge that our research team had, we created a digital collaboration board that included an agenda, problem statement and two ideation exercises. Our goal was to define the problem as a group and set out exploring how we might solve the problem, then draft up some quick sketches to illustrate a solution and share with the group. Participants would then vote on ideas or solutions and all data would be collected and used in the next step. With our digital board all set and two hours blocked off on the calendar, we got started.*

*The two hour design sprint felt a little unnatural at first, as I was accustomed to a longer, more laborious introduction used in a five day design sprint. In my previous experience, we wouldn't advance to a productive part of the sprint until well into the first day and sometimes the second day. In this session, however, participants were eager and excited to contribute, despite never participating in a design sprint before. Our problem statement had gone from being a vague understanding to a complete and concise sentence upon which everyone could agree. With the problem defined, we could now define what a successful outcome looked like.*

*Participants started drafting up potential solutions in "How Might We" statements, using one or two sentences. This exercise requires little effort from the participants but produces tons of value for the design thinking process since these simple statements can continue to build off each other and help to grow ideas further. I was shocked at how quickly our board filled up with ideas and statements with the short 20-30 minutes we had. Participants were encouraged to share their statements while the others asked questions. After everyone had presented, users would vote on statements using digital stickers or emojis. Ideas with the most interactions would be used for our next exercise, which was sketching.*

*Within the first hour of the two hour design sprint, we were light-years ahead of where we had started. We had created a completely synchronous board filled with potential ideas and vetted them down to a handful of key ideas to iterate upon. The participants were encouraged to use any means whatsoever to illustrate their ideas, such as a pad of paper and a pen or their most comfortable software like Microsoft PowerPoint or Word. Once time was up, participants shared their ideas in a similar method used in the previous exercise and we voted on them accordingly. As the sprint came to a close, the facilitators then walked the participants through the asynchronous next steps. After the last participant logged out of our virtual session, I was amazed at what was on the screen in front of me.*

*In a complete digital environment and within two hours, I not only had a better understanding of what was needed to best serve our users, but I also had dozens of additional ideas and actionable solutions in front of me, each fulfilling the goal of the desired feature and addressing our problem statement.*

*The two hour design sprint was a success. Our team now had a clear definition of our problem, goal, and potential solutions. This helped our design team to create prototypes that we could then validate with users and could be added to the next product update. From then on, the two hour design sprint became the preferred method for problem solving. As we continued to run design sprints, we would get more streamlined and efficient and learn how to get even more out of the time we had. We then started extending the design sprints to problems outside of user requests. We would run design sprints for process improvements, communication across teams, and much more. With each design sprint we ran, we also continued to get more and more successful with our solutions. The next steps were more clear and concise and required less meetings and emails for follow up.*

*If you are looking to run your own two hour design sprint, I would advise you to trust the process. You will be amazed at how far an idea can go in such a short amount of time. If you don't feel like you got anywhere at the end of the two hours, I would encourage you to schedule another session and run it again. The more comfortable your participants get with the two hour design sprints, the more they are likely to stay engaged and produce insightful ideas. Before you know it, you will be running more design sprints and producing quality designs and features in a fraction of the time.*

## Ruben Betancourt, Head of Product, Tango.io

*For product managers, it's necessary to ensure that a proposed* solution is technically feasible, easy to use, and meets the end users' needs. One effective approach to achieve these goals is by conducting a one-week design sprint. Although having eight people in one room for a full week can be challenging, it's still a realistic option for co-located teams. However, for distributed teams like ours, it's not feasible to gather stakeholders for that length of time due to the added stress of long video conference calls and potential distractions.

At Tango, we encountered this challenge and created a shorter version of the design sprint to tackle release-level issues, but it was still too time consuming to be implemented at a feature-level due to the lack of availability of product stakeholders and the day-to-day responsibilities of the product team. As a result, we needed to find alternative solutions for our discovery process, which often required multiple rounds of prototyping only to ensure buy-in from everyone involved.

When I heard about the two hour design sprint method, I was immediately intrigued. I was confident that there was a way to save time from the team and stakeholders while still gaining their valuable input. After attending a two hour design sprint workshop, it became clear to me that this was the process I had been looking for.

The first two hour design sprint we ran for one of our products was highly productive. The session allowed everyone to understand the problem from all angles, provide input, and agree on a path forward, all without sacrificing days of work away from their regular activities. Since then, it has become our go-to process for feature-level product discovery.

Two hour design sprints are the perfect solution for engaging product stakeholders who may not be as enthusiastic to participate, but whose buy-in and input is essential for the success of a feature. By incorporating two hour design sprints in every feature-level discovery process we run, we have reduced the time needed to spend in the discovery process for both product stakeholders and team members, while still capturing their valuable input and ensuring early buy-in.

# Alesandro Meléndez, User Experience Designer, TreviPay

*In my personal experience the two hour design sprint method has been instrumental in the successful kickoff for all the design initiatives I've been a part of at TreviPay. It has allowed me, a UX practitioner, to engage with a cross functional team, where all stakeholders are in a focused physical and mental space. This approach allows us to democratize the design thinking process to solve our users' needs.*

*The biggest value I have seen from being part of the two hour design sprint method is being able to crowdsource some amazing solutions from the deep wells of knowledge, experience, and insights of the sprint participants in a short amount of time. My favorite part of the process is seeing the creativity from stakeholders who do not consider themselves "designers." They leave the sprint feeling empowered knowing they had a hand in crafting a great potential solution.*

*My advice to anyone doing their first two hour design sprint is to do as much prep work as possible. If I were to use a cooking analogy, food comes out of a restaurant kitchen faster if all the prep work has been done ahead of time. Also, if that prep work is done well, everyone can focus on delivering consistent, high-quality dishes. So, comparing that to the two hour design sprint method, I would say the same principle applies. If you are the facilitator and do all the "prep work" (such as setting up a good agenda, have the framework for the problem statement, as well as doing the advance work to document stickies of the known pain points), you will certainly cut down on having to deal with the clerical aspects of the sprint, thus allowing you to maximize your time and focus on turning "How Might We" statements into high-quality brainstormed solutions.*

*If I were to compare two hour design sprints with five day design sprints from a holistic UX perspective, I would say the two hour design sprint approach can significantly reduce multiple pain points for the participants and the organization itself. The traditional five day sprint design method can lead to a long week that may end up with reduced engagement, diminished mental focus, and the very real financial impact of having a large group of stakeholders dialed in on one task for a whole week. In contrast, the two hour design sprint method allows for a significant reduction in time and financial investment, while still producing tangible potential solutions. This allows everyone involved to still have the time and energy to complete other important aspects of their duties and responsibilities.*

*Every organization has limited resources and wants to maximize the impact of their work. The two hour sprint session allows for better focus and engagement on the issue at hand. I personally believe the output of the two hour design sprint is comparable to what can be produced from the traditional five day design sprint. Even though at the end of the two hours you don't have a workable prototype that has been validated through some form of testing, I believe the prototyping and testing aspects of the design thinking process can occur outside the confines of the sprint session with little to no impact on the timeline to launch.*

## Diana Stepner, Head of Product, Chan Zuckerberg Initiative

*For a number of companies I've worked with, holding a five day design sprint has required too much time - both to organize and to run. Learning about the two hour design sprint model has opened up opportunities for more teams and companies to explore and approach ideation. The two hour design sprint has provided me with a new approach to encourage and create more opportunities for success by increasing the frequency and shortening the time my organization can explore and solve problems.*

*Through the two hour design sprint model, I have been able to provide my product group with a new and innovative method to rapidly explore small- to medium-sized problems which have typically been sitting in the backlog waiting for an owner. I enjoyed learning about the approach with others and understanding the mechanics of conducting a design sprint as a collaboration between individuals.*

*Reviewing the two hour design sprint resources with the team set everyone up with the right expectations. Given the common foundation, we were able to parse which aspects to cover during the two hour design sprint (reviewing opportunities + user personas, exploring the problem + goals / needs, and ideating solutions that will address the pains / motivations through low fidelity sketches) and afterwards (building prototype solutions and testing with customers). This model enabled us to better include remote team members and experiment + learn even more quickly.*

*Before starting your first two hour design sprint, I recommend individuals ensure there is a common understanding of users and the goals which are being explored. This insight should come from prior user interviews. If this information is not available or there isn't alignment, steps should be taken beforehand to ensure the two hour design sprint is an effective use of time for all involved.*

*The biggest difference compared to traditional five day design sprints for me has been observing how effective the two hour design sprint can be for remote workers. Given the approach and structure, it works extremely well for our hybrid world. With the traditional five day design sprints, even though they can be done remotely, the time commitment tends to make maintaining attention tricky. Also scheduling the customer interviews often requires additional individuals to be included to coordinate the calls and provide support during the five day time frame.*

# Courtney Buchmann, Senior Product Manager, TreviPay

*I am a Product Manager with more than 15 years of experience bringing new software features of all scopes of complexity to market. While I have long recognized the value of design sprints in identifying pain points, understanding the customer journey, and aligning on possible solutions, they often seemed difficult to plan. Even if you can get the right people in the same room, it is challenging to keep participants fully engaged for an entire day. This led to often skipping this important and valuable ceremony, due to the feeling that we can only do a design sprint for very special projects.*

*I have converted to the two hour design sprint model because it is so much easier to plan and execute. A major value to the two hour timeframe is that it allows external end users to participate. They are almost always willing to give us two hours, whereas four to eight hours is unthinkable; forty hours would be impossible.. The inclusion of end user perspectives is valuable, especially for product owners who support industries in which they have very little personal experience.*

*For example, I recently led a two hour design sprint that included administrators and managers from a client in the parts and services sector of the trucking industry. This is a business vertical where, unless you are employed in this industry, you are not going to know much about the roles, daily tasks, and goals that the software needs to support. Understanding the scope of the problem often leads to additional meetings or emails to clarify the issues and extra time is needed to fine tune the solution. By involving the end users who could describe the problem they wanted to solve from the start, they were able to pinpoint the value that certain features would bring and share their vision of success. This allowed the product and UX teams to move very quickly to create high fidelity mockups that needed almost no revisions. Committing to running a design sprint for every project is an important element of success, and the two hour design sprint opens the door for more of these essential ceremonies.*

## Emily Farabi, Manager of Product – Payments & Aviation, TreviPay

*I am very much a Type A personality. I see the goal and I figure out how to achieve it. This can be great in product management, but I also need to be aware of the downsides. It is very easy to overlook important details, miss key elements due to perspective or assumptions, and quickly determine a solution without understanding all possibilities. As I took on a project to redesign our corporate portal, I needed to find a way to quickly achieve our goal, but also make smart, value-driven, and agreeable decisions across many stakeholders and personas. The two hour design sprint allowed us to efficiently and effectively bring a new solution to life.*

*To conduct a successful two hour design sprint, the right type of homework must be done prior to the workshop. We pulled together all relevant information in an easily digestible format. I worked with the team to interview two to three stakeholders from each of our clients. Every client had a different need for the new portal, a specific job to be done, or a pain point that was costing time and money. This feedback was used to outline our personas and categorize into general roles using the platform. We tracked all feedback into jobs to be done, which would later be used to flesh out ideas during our 'How Might We' statements in the workshop. The prep homework also included existing site usage data, survey feedback, and screenshots of various platforms for reference. The more artifacts we could provide upfront in the workshop, the more informed the participants could be in their contributions.*

*In the first part of the workshop, we reviewed all collected data and interview feedback. This is how we get to know the consumer and empathize with their needs. We used the second part of the workshop to outline potential solutions, or 'How Might We' statements. Instead of thinking about what product we would create, it helped us to think about what we will solve. The group voted on all possible solutions to get an idea of where the most value could be provided to our consumers.*

*Because we took time getting to know our consumers in the first part of the workshop, the voting process was driven from facts and feedback instead of assumptions. The really fun part of the workshop is the last part – the solution sketching. We each worked independently to design the 'How Might We' problem for which we were solving and come up with the best tools to get the job done. This is where the magic of many minds happens. In our workshop, several unique ideas were presented and cool details were drawn out of the research and transformed into a sketch. We then voted on sketches and talked about what we really liked.*

*It was so wonderful to see all of these thoughts come together! We could take ideas from each sketch and incorporate them into our final design. My perspective had been broadened and I was excited!*

*So, we were able to funnel stakeholder feedback, data, solutions, ideas, feedback, brainstorming, creativity, perspectives, and new ideas into a combined concept for our corporate portal. We did this in two hours instead of one to two weeks and we came out with a better design with input from all. It was effective, it was efficient, and every participant was key in making it happen. This is my kind of design sprint!*

## Brian Cox, Founder and CEO, Digital Bullpen

*For starters, remember why you are using the design sprint process: you want to be a design-driven product company. For these types of institutions, the two hour design sprint is a great tool to use in the early stages when building out a new feature or user experience for your product. It creates an opportunity to get key stakeholders in a room to bring their unique perspectives and context that will inform the project.*

*The process creates space to surface problems, acknowledges technological constraints, and aligns your team. In my experience, even the people who claim to be the least creative provide some of the best solutions. As the team unpacks the intended problem, it naturally surfaces additional and even adjacent problems that would have a greater impact on business. This discovery often comes with more refined, cost-effective solutions that don't require as much time or resources to deliver. What a win for your team! More evidence that this process works.*

*Design-led companies need tools that solve big problems, otherwise, they won't use them. And frankly, why would you want to if it doesn't work? Companies of all sizes need to solve problems with the most impact but struggle to commit leadership resources for traditional design sprints. Buy-in is a fringe benefit of the shorter time commitment, but focus from the entire team is the fuel that gives life to this creative engine. To encourage confidence in the process from leadership it has been helpful to have a clear agenda teed up beforehand, focused exercises, and a desired outcome that espouses a business metric that matters to the company. Inability to include your key subject matter experts in the room is like paddling a boat with one oar, you'll just be going in circles or perhaps never arrive at the desired destination.*

*Resist the urge to celebrate the success of running a great design sprint in and of itself, it is a trap. The work has just begun. The ultimate goal of any design sprint practitioner must be to harvest the fruits of the design sprint. So, be sure to assign deliverables and a timeline to implement the solution. This will help to cement the usage of this strategy as a part of solving business problems in a design-driven company. Many great creative solutions die on the vine without an execution strategy. The two hour design sprint process is an efficient, effective, and valuable tool to help design-led product companies solve big problems.*

## Angela Skalberg-Mander, Manager, Platform Products, TreviPay

*Anything that involves a large amount of people is costly. Afterall, time is money. Traditional design sprints require multiple days to run the process successfully. Participants must push pause on their daily activities to be available. The cost goes beyond the participation in the design sprint. Unintentional added stress comes from the time away from their daily activities and the pressure to catch up with missed work. This might dissuade participation altogether.*

*In product and technology, we strive to be agile. We ideate and move fast. Traditional design sprints tend to fall short of agile. But what if we could focus two hours collaborating to identify your focus? How could that improve the discovery process? It allows for more participation, less impact to daily activities, and decreases time between discovery and development. It becomes complementary to agile development. My experience with participating in two hour design sprints has been enlightening. I have seen a greater amount of participation that led to action-driven results. It captures and retains each individual's attention and focus. Participants feel more comfortable expressing their ideas and opinions. It induces confidence and trust between product management and participants. As product managers, we reap the benefit of quick results, instilled confidence, and a path forward with two hour design sprints.*

# ON-DEMAND TRAINING FOR TWO HOUR DESIGN SPRINTS

**Udemy Course**[1]

**2 Hour Design Sprints: Learn How to Solve Problems and Design Products in Just 2 Hours vs. 5 Days Using Figma FigJam**

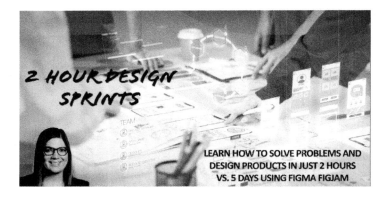

**What's Included:**

Receive the tools and a step-by-step guide on running your own two hour design sprint:

- Over 90 minutes of training videos

- Two hour design sprint Figma FigJam template live demo

- Demonstration on how to setup and conduct a two hour design sprint

- Resources, tips, and tools

- Udemy Course Certificate of Completion

# Figma FigJam Template[2]

## 2 Hour Design Sprints

This template is a free guide for readers of *"Solving Problems in 2 Hours: How to Brainstorm and Create Solutions with Two Hour Design Sprints"* or users of the on-demand training *"2 Hour Design Sprints: Learn how to solve problems and design products in just 2 hours vs. 5 days using Figma FigJam,"* or anyone just looking to adapt a two hour design sprint model using Figma FigJam.

# *ABOUT BILL STAIKOS*

With more than 25 years in financial services and a primary focus on driving customer and employee experience excellence, Bill is a recognized client advocate with proven expertise in envisioning and executing holistic customer-centric strategies.

He is currently Senior Vice President, Executive Advisory for Medallia, the leader in enterprise experience management software. Bill also hosts an award-winning, weekly podcast, Be Customer Led, with listeners in 110 countries, focused on helping Customer and Employee Experience practitioners accelerate their careers, and defining the future of user experience.

Bill has expertise in customer and employee research and insights, data and analytics, UX strategy, design, transformation, and leveraging artificial intelligence *(AI)* and machine learning to make better decisions in creating a customer-led culture. Bill holds a BS in Business from the State University of New York at Oswego and an MBA from New York University's Stern School of Business. He has also served as a volunteer and board member for the Princeton Nursery School, Westwood Country Club, Fast Company Executive Board and as a mentor for startups through 76 Forward.

# *ABOUT JOHN KILLE*

John Kille, Ph.D. is a UX researcher, strategist, and designer, as well as a writer and speaker with over 15 years experience in the UX industry. John leads UX research, strategy, and design at TreviPay, a global B2B payments and invoicing network.

A former journalist and college professor, John has led extensive user-centered design and customer research projects in the usability lab, online, and in the field across the U.S. and in countries such as India, Germany, England, and the Netherlands. He also regularly speaks at UX conferences and continues to publish in places such as UXPA Magazine and UXMatters.com.

John holds a BA in Psychology and English from Rockhurst University, an MA in English *(focused in Sociolinguistics)* from the University of Minnesota, and a PhD in Cultural Studies *(focused in ethnography and human group behavior)* from St. Louis University. He also served on the Advisory Board in 2022 for Missouri State University's Design Thinking program.

# *CONTRIBUTORS*

**Collin Williamson, Senior UX Designer, TreviPay**
Collin is an experienced designer with nearly a decade of experience being a visionary and creative thinker in solving problems for users with design, and understanding the wants and needs of users, including a focus on compliance and best practices for users of all needs and wants.

**Ruben Betancourt, Head of Product, Tango.io**
Ruben is a product leader with a vision for redefining product management approaches, product discovery and product delivery as part of the product management standards including the management of teams, complex products and successful delivery of innovative solutions on time.

**Alesandro Meléndez, User Experience Designer, TreviPay**
Alesandro is a user experience designer with a background in fine art, human services, and education who believes understanding the wants, needs and struggles of others is the key to brilliant design and meaningful change and has allowed him to develop a strength-based creative approach towards problem solving.

**Diana Stepner, Head of Product, Chan Zuckerberg Initiative**
Diana is a product leader who creates a strong culture of learning and success, empowering multidisciplinary teams to adopt an

experimentation and outcome driven mindset and who thrives on building collaborative teams, leading innovation efforts, and using qualitative + quantitative insights to establish product goals and achieve growth.

**Courtney Buchmann, Senior Product Manager, TreviPay**
Courtney is an experienced product owner and product manager that enjoys facilitating initial strategic visions of projects through obtaining internal stakeholder feedback, customer interviews, competitive analysis and seeing projects from development through beta testing, and continued support of clients and customers after the launch.

**Emily Farabi, Manager of Product – Payments & Aviation, TreviPay**
Emily is an experienced product leader with a background in project management and enjoys helping to turn customer visions into reality through executing on tactical strategies for customer solutions that fulfill the needs of the customer journey and user needs and wants.

**Brian Cox, Founder and CEO, Digital Bullpen**
Brian is an energetic and highly motivated founder and CEO with over a decade of experience in product design and leadership roles. His creative thinking is aimed at solutions that will move a business towards their goals on time and on budget.
Angela Skalberg-Mander, Manager, Platform Products, TreviPay
Angela is a tenacious product leader with a background in product management and psychology with deep knowledge of the financial services industry and a focus on managing complex products and building high-performance product teams.

# *ABOUT TERESA CAIN*

Teresa is an author, speaker, entrepreneur and technology executive with over 15 years overseeing global product and user experience teams. Teresa has diverse experience leading product management, product design, research, strategy and innovation for digital solutions and as a consultant for startup technology firms.

Teresa is the Director of Product, UX and Design at TreviPay, where she drives vision, strategy and UX for multiple FinTech products and teams. She is the Founder of Lucid Startup Consulting where she coaches startups. Teresa serves as an advisor for Central Exchange, a women's nonprofit, and on the board of DevStride, a project and portfolio management solution.

Teresa regularly speaks at conferences on design thinking, customer experience, and product innovation. Teresa received a prestigious Emerging Scholar Award in 2023 from the International Conference on Design Principles and Practices including presenting on her research *"Putting Into Practice Evolving Design Thinking Methods at Technology Firms: The Evolution To 2 Hour Design Sprints."* She is also a 2022 Women in IT Summit & Award Series Finalist for Advocate of the Year.

Teresa has completed many certifications during her career

in product, customer experience, agile, project management and process management including Pragmatic Marketing Certified III ©, Net Promoter Certified Associate, Certified Scrum Product Owner, Certified Scrum Master, Project Management Professional and Lean Six Sigma Green Belt. She also completed Northwestern University's Kellogg School of Management Executive Program for Product Strategy methods, a program with a focus on discovering, developing, managing and marketing products as a business.

Teresa earned a BS in Journalism from the William Allen White School of Journalism and a BA in English from the University of Kansas. She earned an Executive MBA from Rockhurst University and is studying a second Master's degree in Integrated Innovation for Products and Services at Carnegie Mellon University, focusing on product and user experience design principles.

## Connect with Teresa Cain online:

https://www.2hourdesignsprints.com
https://www.linkedin.com/in/cainteresa/

# *ENDNOTES*

## Preface

1.    Centers for Disease Control and Prevention. *(n.d.).*
      *2009 H1N1 Pandemic (H1N1pdm09 virus).* Retrieved
      March 5, 2023 from https://www.cdc.gov/flu/pandem-
      ic-resources/2009-h1n1-pandemic.html

2.    Centers for Disease Control and Prevention. *(n.d.).*
      *2014-2016 Ebola Outbreak in West Africa.* Retrieved
      March 5, 2023 from https://www.cdc.gov/vhf/ebola/
      history/2014-2016-outbreak/index.html

3.    Centers for Disease Control and Prevention. *(n.d.)*
      *Zika Virus.* Retrieved March 5, 2023 from https://
      www.cdc.gov/zika/index.html

## Introduction

1.    Balle, L. *(n.d.). Information on Small Business Startups.*
      Retrieved March 7, 2023. https://smallbusiness.chron.
      com/information-small-business-startups-2491.html

2.    Hamel, G., & Valikangas, L. *(2003, September 1). The
      quest for resilience.* Harvard Business Review. Retrieved
      March 6, 2023, from https://hbr.org/2003/09/the-
      quest-for-resilience

## Chapter 1: What are Two Hour Design Sprints?

1.    O'Donoghue, J. *(2023, January 14). The Stanford Design Thinking process.* Make. Retrieved March 7, 2023, from https://makeiterate.com/the-stanford-design-thinking-process/

2.    Knapp, J., Zeratsky, J., Kowitz, B., *(2016). Sprint: Solve big problems and test new ideas in just five days.* Simon & Schuster.

3.    Knapp, J., Zeratsky, J., & Kowitz, B. *(2016). Sprint: Solve big problems and test new ideas in just five days.* Simon & Schuster.

4.    *Official 5-Day Design Sprint Template & example for teams: Miro.* https://miro.com/. *(n.d.).* Retrieved March 7, 2023, from https://miro.com/templates/official-remote-5-day-design-sprint/

5.    *The Official Remote Design Sprint Template.* MURAL. *(n.d.).* Retrieved March 7, 2023, from https://www.mural.co/templates/the-official-remote-design-sprint-template

6.    *Design sprint template: Invision Freehand.* invisionapp, inc. *(n.d.).* Retrieved March 7, 2023, from https://www.invisionapp.com/freehand/templates/detail/design-sprint-template

7.    Knapp, J., Zeratsky, J., & Colburn, J. *(n.d.). The Remote Design Sprint Guide.* The Sprint Book. Retrieved March 7, 2023, from https://www.thesprintbook.com/articles/remote-design-sprint-guide

8.    Knapp, J., Zeratsky, J., & Colburn, J. *(n.d.). The Remote Design Sprint Guide.* The Sprint Book. Retrieved

March 7, 2023, from https://www.thesprintbook.com/articles/remote-design-sprint-guide

9. Knapp, J., Zeratsky, J., Kowitz, B., *(2016). Sprint: Solve big problems and test new ideas in just five days.* Simon & Schuster.

10. *One platform to connect.* Zoom. *(n.d.).* Retrieved March 7, 2023, from https://zoom.us/

11. *The visual collaboration platform for every team: Miro.* https://miro.com/. *(n.d.).* Retrieved March 7, 2023, from https://miro.com/

12. *Project Management Software, online collaboration.* Basecamp. *(n.d.).* Retrieved March 7, 2023, from https://basecamp.com/

13. *The user research recruiting platform for teams.* User Interviews. *(n.d.).* Retrieved March 7, 2023, from https://www.userinterviews.com/

14. *Gotomeeting Video Conferencing & Online Meeting Software.* GoTo. *(n.d.).* Retrieved March 7, 2023, from https://www.goto.com/meeting

15. *AJ&SMart – better products, faster.* AJ&Smart –. *(n.d.).* Retrieved March 7, 2023, from https://www.ajsmart.com/

16. *Video meetings, video conferencing and video call API.* Whereby. *(n.d.).* Retrieved March 7, 2023, from https://whereby.com/

17. AJ&SMart – better products, faster. AJ&Smart –. *(n.d.).* Retrieved March 7, 2023, from https://www.ajsmart.com/

## Chapter 2: Solve Any Problem

1. Pipeline Entrepreneurs. *(n.d.).* Retrieved March 7, 2023, from https://www.pipelineentrepreneurs.com/

2. MassChallenge. *(2023, March 6).* Retrieved March 7, 2023, from https://masschallenge.org/

3. *Usertesting human insight platform: improve customer experience (CX).* UserTesting. Retrieved March 7, 2023, from https://www.usertesting.com/

4. *The user research recruiting platform for teams.* User Interviews. *(n.d.).* Retrieved March 7, 2023, from https://www.userinterviews.com/

5. Rehkopf, M. *(n.d.). What Are Sprints.* Atlassian. Retrieved March 7, 2023, from https://www.atlassian.com/agile/about/max-rehkopf

6. Rehkopf, M. *(n.d.). Epics.* Atlassian. Retrieved March 7, 2023, from https://www.atlassian.com/agile/project-management/epics

7. Faller, P. *(2017, October 23). Putting personas to work in UX design: What they are and why they're important.* LaptrinhX. Retrieved March 7, 2023, from https://laptrinhx.com/putting-personas-to-work-in-ux-design-what-they-are-and-why-they-re-important-4204952394/

8. *Design Sprint Ltd, experts of the google design sprint.* Design Sprint. *(2023, January 24).* Retrieved March 7, 2023, from https://design-sprint.com/

9. AJ&Smart. *(n.d.). Design sprint masterclass by AJ&SMart.* Design Sprint Masterclass by AJ&Smart. Retrieved March 7, 2023, from https://ajsmart.com/

masterclass

10. *What are design sprints?: Design Sprint Basics.* Udacity. *(n.d.).* Retrieved March 7, 2023, from https://www.udacity.com/course/design-sprint-foundations-nanodegree--nd201

11. Knapp, J., Zeratsky, J., & Kowitz, B. *(2016). Sprint: Solve big problems and test new ideas in just five days.* Simon & Schuster.

12. Knapp, J., Zeratsky, & Colburn. *(n.d.). The design sprint.* The Sprint Book. Retrieved March 7, 2023, from https://www.thesprintbook.com/the-design-sprint

13. Banfield, R., Lombardo, C. T., Wax, T., & Gray, D. *(2017). Design sprint: A practical guidebook for building great digital products.* O'Reilly Media, Inc.

14. Pinheiro, T. *(2018, February 13). The GV Model Guide: A Guide for Google Ventures' design sprint: Paperback.* Barnes & Noble. Retrieved March 5, 2023, from https://www.barnesandnoble.com/w/the-gv-model-guide-tenny-pinheiro/1129654996

15. *The Online Collaborative Whiteboard for teams.* Figma FigJam. *(n.d.).* Retrieved March 7, 2023, from https://www.figma.com/figjam/

16. Win, J. *(2017, July 14). 2- hour sprint for busy stakeholders.* Medium. Retrieved March 5, 2023, from https://justinewin.medium.com/2-hour-sprint-for-busy-stakeholders-bb2a5ad07507

17. Illuk, C. *(2017, November 18). The 2 hour design sprint.* Medium. Retrieved March 7, 2023, from https://blog.prototypr.io/the-2-hour-design-sprint-9e2bbc14ee1

18.   Google. *(n.d.). Share and engage with the design sprint community.* Google. Retrieved March 7, 2023, from https://designsprintkit.withgoogle.com/methodology/phase3-sketch/crazy-8s

19.   *Lessons learnt from a 2-hour design sprint.* Fabric Group: A Global Partner delivering outcomes for you. *(n.d.).* Retrieved March 7, 2023, from https://www.fabricgroup.com.au/blog/lessons-learnt-from-a-2-hour-design-sprint

20.   Katalinich Follow Director, B. *(n.d.). 2-Hour design sprint agenda.* Share and Discover Knowledge on SlideShare. Retrieved March 5, 2023, from https://www.slideshare.net/brookecreef/2hour-design-sprint-agenda-115041412

21.   Ganón, M. *(2022, May 30). Designing an onboarding experience in a 2-hour design sprint.* Medium. Retrieved March 5, 2023, from https://blog.zeppelinlabs.io/designing-an-onboarding-experience-in-a-2-hour-design-sprint-fbb55987dfbe

## Chapter 3: Evolution of the Design Sprint

1.   McKim, R. H. *(1980, January 1). Experiences in visual thinking, 2nd edition.* AbeBooks. Retrieved March 7, 2023, from https://www.abebooks.com/9780818504112/Experiences-Visual-Thinking-2nd-edition-0818504110/plp

2.   *IDEO design thinking.* IDEO. *(n.d.).* Retrieved March 7, 2023, from https://designthinking.ideo.com/

3.   Stanford d.school. *(n.d.).* Retrieved March 7, 2023, from https://dschool.stanford.edu/

4.   Knapp, J., Zeratsky, & Colburn. *(n.d.). The design sprint*. The Sprint Book. Retrieved March 7, 2023, from https://www.thesprintbook.com/the-design-sprint

5.   Knapp, J., Zeratsky, J., & Kowitz, B. *(2016). Sprint: Solve big problems and test new ideas in just five days*. Simon & Schuster.

6.   Grantham-Philips, W. *(2023, January 20)*. Google to lay off 12,000 employees, the latest tech giant to cut thousands of Jobs. USA Today. Retrieved March 7, 2023, from https://www.usatoday.com/story/money/2023/01/20/google-layoffs-jobs-employees-cut/11088409002/

7.   Wonder. *(n.d.)*. Retrieved March 7, 2023, from https://askwonder.com/research/statistics-tech-work-force-us-employees-work-private-companies-public-companies-1rhgo54r5

8.   *One platform to connect*. Zoom. *(n.d.)*. Retrieved March 7, 2023, from https://zoom.us/

## Chapter 4: History of UX

1.   Nielsen, J. *(n.d.). A 100-year view of user experience (by Jakob Nielsen)*. Nielsen Norman Group. Retrieved March 7, 2023, from https://www.nngroup.com/articles/100-years-ux/

2.   White, C. *(2019, September 8). Do not confuse user experience with customer experience*. Usability Geek. Retrieved March 7, 2023, from https://usabilitygeek.com/confuse-user-experience-customer-experience/

3.   *Qualtrics announces definitive agreement to acquire Clarabridge*. Qualtrics. *(2022, September 15)*. Retrieved

March 7, 2023, from https://www.qualtrics.com/news/
qualtrics-announces-definitive-agreement-to-acquire-
clarabridge/

4.  *NPS methodology.* NICE Satmetrix. *(2022, January 5).*
    Retrieved March 7, 2023, from https://www.satmetrix.
    com/holistic-voc-solution/nps-methodology/

5.  Medallia. *(n.d.). Experience management software plat-
    form.* Medallia. Retrieved March 7, 2023, from https://
    www.medallia.com/

6.  *The customer company.* Salesforce. *(n.d.).* Retrieved
    March 7, 2023, from https://www.salesforce.com/

7.  SMG. *(2023, January 9).* Retrieved March 7, 2023,
    from https://smg.com/

8.  *Qualtrics announces definitive agreement to acquire
    Clarabridge.* Qualtrics. *(2022, September 15).* Retrieved
    March 7, 2023, from https://www.qualtrics.com/news/
    qualtrics-announces-definitive-agreement-to-acquire-
    clarabridge/

9.  *The world's most popular free online survey tool.* Survey-
    Monkey. *(n.d.).* Retrieved March 7, 2023, from https://
    www.surveymonkey.com/

10. Kelly, J. *(2023, February 7). If companies follow the lead
    of Elon Musk and Mark Zuckerberg, middle managers
    are the next layoff victims.* Forbes. Retrieved March
    7, 2023, from https://www.forbes.com/sites/jack-
    kelly/2023/02/06/if-companies-follow-the-lead-of-elon-
    musk-and-mark-zuckerberg-middle-managers-are-the-
    next-layoff-victims/?sh=4af2707c758f

11. Weinberger, M. *(n.d.). Mark Zuckerberg just ushered*

*in a new era of Tech, where profitability and efficiency trump perks and culture.* Business Insider. Retrieved March 7, 2023, from https://www.businessinsider.com/mark-zuckerberg-meta-facebook-new-era-efficiency-2023-2

12. Hecht, E. *(2023, February 9). What years are gen X? what about baby boomers? when each generation was born.* USA Today. Retrieved March 7, 2023, from https://www.usatoday.com/story/news/2022/09/02/what-years-gen-x-millennials-baby-boomers-gen-z/10303085002/

13. *Understanding generation alpha.* McCrindle. *(2023, March 6).* Retrieved March 7, 2023, from https://mccrindle.com.au/article/topic/generation-alpha/generation-alpha-defined/

14. Bonthuys, D. *(2021, August 23). The Super Nintendo Entertainment System is officially 30 Years Old Today.* GameSpot. Retrieved March 7, 2023, from https://www.gamespot.com/articles/the-super-nintendo-entertainment-system-is-officially-30-years-old-today/1100-6495438/

15. *List of super nintendo entertainment system games.* Nintendo. *(n.d.).* Retrieved March 7, 2023, from https://nintendo.fandom.com/wiki/List_of_Super_Nintendo_Entertainment_System_games

16. Bonthuys, D. *(2021, August 23). The Super Nintendo Entertainment System is officially 30 Years Old Today.* GameSpot. Retrieved March 7, 2023, from https://www.gamespot.com/articles/the-super-nintendo-entertainment-system-is-officially-30-years-old-today/1100-6495438/

17. *Game boy.* National Museum of American History. *(n.d.).* Retrieved March 7, 2023, from https://americanhistory.si.edu/collections/search/object/nmah_1253117

18. *15 years of WIFI - a timeline - fon: The global WIFI Network.* Fon. *(2018, May 28).* Retrieved March 7, 2023, from https://fon.com/fon-wifi-infographic/

## Chapter 5: Impact of Remote Work on Design Sprints

1. Wells, M. *(2019, June 27). Here's how much Silicon Valley Tech workers actually make.* SFGATE. Retrieved March 7, 2023, from https://www.sfgate.com/tech/article/Silicon-Valley-tech-workers-companies-salary-pay-14047115.php

2. *11 awesome google benefits and perks for employees.* PerkUp. *(n.d.).* Retrieved March 7, 2023, from https://www.perkupapp.com/post/11-awesome-google-benefits-and-perks-for-employees

3. Grantham-Philips, W. *(2023, January 20). Google to lay off 12,000 employees, the latest tech giant to cut thousands of Jobs.* USA Today. Retrieved March 7, 2023, from https://www.usatoday.com/story/money/2023/01/20/google-layoffs-jobs-employees-cut/11088409002/

4. Scholes, L. *(n.d.). Sprinting ahead - library.* Google Design. Retrieved March 7, 2023, from https://design.google/library/design-sprints/

5. Scholes, L. *(n.d.). Sprinting ahead - library.* Google Design. Retrieved March 7, 2023, from https://design.google/library/design-sprints/

6.    Stanford d.school. *(n.d.).* Retrieved March 7, 2023, from https://dschool.stanford.edu/

7.    Knapp, J., Zeratsky, J., & Kowitz, B. *(2016). Sprint: Solve big problems and test new ideas in just five days.* Simon & Schuster.

8.    *Collaborate better: Invision.* invisionapp, inc. *(n.d.).* Retrieved March 7, 2023, from https://www.invisionapp.com/

9.    *The visual collaboration platform for every team: Miro.* https://miro.com/. *(n.d.).* Retrieved March 7, 2023, from https://miro.com/

10.   *The Online Collaborative Whiteboard for teams.* Figma FigJam. *(n.d.).* Retrieved March 7, 2023, from https://www.figma.com/figjam/

11.   Torres, J. *(2022, September 27). How does Adobe's $20B acquisition of Figma Impact UX designers?* CMSWire. com. Retrieved March 7, 2023, from https://www.cmswire.com/digital-experience/how-does-adobes-20b-acquisition-of-figma-impact-ux-designers/

12.   *One platform to connect.* Zoom. *(n.d.).* Retrieved March 7, 2023, from https://zoom.us/

13.   *Make it a Mural Not just a Meeting. Mural. (n.d.)* Retrieved March 7, 2023 from https://www.mural.co

14.   Torres, J. *(2022, September 27). How does Adobe's $20B acquisition of Figma Impact UX designers?* CMSWire. com. Retrieved March 7, 2023, from https://www.cmswire.com/digital-experience/how-does-adobes-20b-acquisition-of-figma-impact-ux-designers/

15.   Kunert, Paul. *(2023, February 24).Uncle Sam to block*

*Adobe absorption of Figma over monopoly fears. The Register.* Retrieved March 9, 2023, from https://www.theregister.com/2023/02/24/doj_to_block_adobe_purchase/

16. *Make. Create. Amazing.* Adobe Creative Cloud. *(n.d.)* Retrieved March 7, 2023 from https://www.adobe.com/creativecloud.html

17. *2 hour design sprints: Figma community.* Figma. *(n.d.).* Retrieved March 7, 2023, from https://www.figma.com/community/file/1199463622528181509

## Interlude: The Importance of Discovery Research Before the Two Hour Design Sprint by John Kille

1. Knapp, J., Zeratsky, J., & Kowitz, B. *(2016). Sprint: Solve big problems and test new ideas in just five days.* Simon & Schuster.

2. Klein, L. *(2018). Ux for lean startups: Faster, Smarter User Experience Research and Design.* O'Reilly Media, Inc.

3. *One platform to connect.* Zoom. *(n.d.).* Retrieved March 7, 2023, from https://zoom.us/

4. *Microsoft teams.* Video Conferencing, Meetings, Calling. *(n.d.).* Retrieved March 7, 2023, from https://www.microsoft.com/en-us/microsoft-teams/group-chat-software

5. Google. *(n.d.). Analytics Tools & Solutions for your business.* Google Analytics. Retrieved March 7, 2023, from https://marketingplatform.google.com/about/analytics/

6. *Product Analytics & Event Tracking Platform.* Ampli-

tude. *(n.d.).* Retrieved March 7, 2023, from https://amplitude.com/

7.   *Lucky Orange Heatmaps, recordings, surveys: Conversion funnel tools.* Lucky Orange Heatmaps, Recordings, Surveys | Conversion Funnel Tools. *(n.d.).* Retrieved March 7, 2023, from https://www.luckyorange.com/

8.   *Website heatmaps & behavior analytics tools.* Hotjar. *(n.d.).* Retrieved March 7, 2023, from https://www.hotjar.com/

9.   *2 hour design sprints: Figma community.* Figma. *(n.d.).* Retrieved March 7, 2023, from https://www.figma.com/community/file/1199463622528181509

10.   *NPS methodology.* NICE Satmetrix. *(2022, January 5).* Retrieved March 7, 2023, from https://www.satmetrix.com/holistic-voc-solution/nps-methodology/

11.   Cooper, A. *(1999, January 1). The inmates are running The asylum (1999 edition).* Open Library. Retrieved March 5, 2023, from https://openlibrary.org/books/OL52849M/The_inmates_are_running_the_asylum

12.   *2 hour design sprints*: Figma community. Figma. *(n.d.).* Retrieved March 7, 2023, from https://www.figma.com/community/file/1199463622528181509

13.   *2 hour design sprints*: Figma community. Figma. *(n.d.).* Retrieved March 7, 2023, from https://www.figma.com/community/file/1199463622528181509

## Chapter 6: Stage 1 Empathize with Customers (30 minutes)

1.   *Focus.* Spotify. *(n.d.).* Retrieved March 7, 2023, from https://open.spotify.com/?

2. *2 hour design sprints*: Figma community. Figma. *(n.d.)*. Retrieved March 7, 2023, from https://www.figma. com/community/file/1199463622528181509

## Chapter 7: Stage 2 Explore the Problem (30 minutes)

1. Rosala, M. *(n.d.)*. *Using "how might we" questions to ideate on the right problems*. Nielsen Norman Group. Retrieved March 7, 2023, from https://www.nngroup. com/articles/how-might-we-questions/

2. Rosala, M. *(n.d.)*. *Using "how might we" questions to ideate on the right problems*. Nielsen Norman Group. Retrieved March 7, 2023, from https://www.nngroup. com/articles/how-might-we-questions/

3. Rosala, M. *(n.d.)*. *Using "how might we" questions to ideate on the right problems*. Nielsen Norman Group. Retrieved March 7, 2023, from https://www.nngroup. com/articles/how-might-we-questions/

4. *Watch*. Apple. *(n.d.)*. Retrieved March 7, 2023, from https://www.apple.com/watch/

5. *Salesforce CRM: Everything you need to know. (n.d.)*. Salesforce. Retrieved March 7, 2023, from https:// www.salesforce.com/crm/

6. *CRM Dynamics 365. (n.d.)*. Microsoft. Retrieved March 7, 2023, from https://dynamics.microsoft.com/ en-us/crm/what-is-crm/

7. Google. *(n.d.)*. *Analytics Tools & Solutions for your business*. *Google Analytics*. Retrieved March 7, 2023, from https://marketingplatform.google.com/about/analytics/

8. *Product Analytics & Event Tracking Platform*. Ampli-

tude. *(n.d.)*. Retrieved March 7, 2023, from https://amplitude.com/

9. Medallia. *(n.d.)*. *Experience management software platform.* Medallia. Retrieved March 7, 2023, from https://www.medallia.com/

10. *Qualtrics XM - experience management software.* Qualtrics. *(2023, March 2).* Retrieved March 7, 2023, from https://www.qualtrics.com/

11. *Introducing chatgpt.* Introducing ChatGPT. *(n.d.).* Retrieved March 7, 2023, from https://openai.com/blog/chatgpt

12. Sarig, M. *(2023, January 16).* *Moti Sarig on linkedin: #ux #designers #research #ai #userexperience #usecases #userstories...: 181 comments.* Moti Sarig on LinkedIn: #ux #designers #research #ai #userexperience #usecases #userstories... | 181 comments. Retrieved March 6, 2023, from https://www.linkedin.com/feed/update/urn:li:activity:7020645822706950144?updateEntityUrn=urn%3Ali%3Afs_feedUpdate%3A%28V2%2Curn%3Ali%3Aactivity%3A7020645822706950144%29

13. Vincent, J. *(2023, January 11).* *OpenAI opens waitlist for 'experimental' paid version of CHATGPT with faster answers.* The Verge. Retrieved March 7, 2023, from https://www.theverge.com/2023/1/11/23549821/openai-professional-experimental-paid-version-waitlist-monetization

14. *What is an API?* Red Hat - We make open source technologies for the enterprise. *(n.d.).* Retrieved March 7, 2023, from https://www.redhat.com/en/topics/api/what-are-application-programming-interfaces

15. *What is natural language processing?* IBM. *(n.d.)*. Retrieved March 7, 2023, from https://www.ibm.com/topics/natural-language-processing

16. Cain, T. *(2023, January 25)*. *Voice of the customer then + now: An evolution of text analytics.* Medium. Retrieved March 7, 2023, from https://teresa-cain.medium.com/voice-of-the-customer-then-now-an-evolution-of-text-analytics-562674fa4349

17. *IBM Watson.* IBM. *(n.d.)*. Retrieved March 7, 2023, from https://www.ibm.com/watson

18. Google. *(n.d.)*. *Cloud translation | google cloud.* Google. Retrieved March 7, 2023, from https://cloud.google.com/translate

19. Nielsen, J. *(n.d.)*. *A 100-year view of user experience.* Nielsen Norman Group. Retrieved March 7, 2023, from https://www.nngroup.com/articles/100-years-ux/

20. Cain, T. *(2023, January 25)*. *Text analytics helps you do more than just listen.* Medium. Retrieved March 7, 2023, from https://teresa-cain.medium.com/text-analytics-helps-you-do-more-than-just-listen-5a327987f10c

21. Gow, G. *(2023, February 13)*. *If chatgpt can disrupt google in 2023, what about your company?* Forbes. Retrieved March 7, 2023, from https://www.forbes.com/sites/glenngow/2023/02/09/if-chatgpt-can-disrupt-google-in-2023-what-about-your-company/?sh=26ba0c2a4d39

# Chapter 8: Stage 3 Ideate Solutions (60 minutes)

1.   Balsamiq Cloud. *(n.d.)*. Retrieved March 7, 2023, from https://balsamiq.cloud/

2.   *The Collaborative Interface Design Tool*. Figma. *(n.d.)*. Retrieved March 7, 2023, from https://www.figma.com/

3.   *The Online Collaborative Whiteboard for teams*. Figma FigJam. *(n.d.)*. Retrieved March 7, 2023, from https://www.figma.com/figjam/

4.   Wujec, T. *(n.d.)*. Tom Wujec: Got a wicked problem? First, tell me how you make toast*(n.d.)*. Retrieved March 7, 2023, from https://www.wickedproblemsolver.com/blog-2/blog-post-title-one-3jfbl

5.   Wujec, T. *(n.d.)*. Tom Wujec: Got a wicked problem? First, tell me how you make toast | TED Talk. Retrieved March 5, 2023, from https://www.ted.com/talks/tom_wujec_got_a_wicked_problem_first_tell_me_how_you_make_toast

6.   *Integrated Innovation Institute Engineering + Design + Business*. Carnegie Mellon University. *(n.d.)*. Retrieved March 7, 2023, from https://www.cmu.edu/iii/on-campus-degrees/miips/index.html

7.   *Integrated Innovation Institute Product Design Innovation Online Certificate*. Carnegie Mellon University. *(n.d.)*. Retrieved March 7, 2023, from https://www.cmu.edu/iii/online-programs/certificates/product-design-innovation.html

## Chapter 9: Stage 4 & 5 Prototype and Test

1.   Balsamiq Cloud. *(n.d.)*. Retrieved March 7, 2023, from https://balsamiq.cloud/

2. Sketch. *(n.d.).* Retrieved March 7, 2023, from https://www.sketch.com/

3. *Collaborate better: Invision.* invisionapp, inc. *(n.d.).* Retrieved March 7, 2023, from https://www.invisionapp.com/

4. *The Collaborative Interface Design Tool.* Figma. *(n.d.).* Retrieved March 7, 2023, from https://www.figma.com/

5. *User Experience Consulting & usability research firm.* Blink. *(n.d.).* Retrieved March 7, 2023, from https://blinkux.com/

6. Journal, W. S. *(n.d.). Y Media Labs: Digital Product & Innovation Agency.* YML. Retrieved March 7, 2023, from https://yml.co/

7. *We design market-ready SAAS Brands.* Digital Bullpen. *(n.d.).* Retrieved March 7, 2023, from https://www.callbullpen.com/

8. *Explore the world's leading design portfolios.* Dribbble. *(n.d.).* Retrieved March 7, 2023, from https://dribbble.com/

9. 99designs. *(n.d.). Logos, web, graphic design & more.* 99designs. Retrieved March 7, 2023, from http://99designs.com/

10. *Fiverr - Freelance Services Marketplace. (n.d.).* Retrieved March 7, 2023, from https://www.fiverr.com/

11. *Online courses - learn anything, on your schedule.* Udemy. *(n.d.).* Retrieved March 7, 2023, from https://www.udemy.com/

12. Cain, T. *(2023, March 6). 2 hour design sprints.* Udemy. Retrieved March 6, 2023, from https://www.udemy.com/course/2hourdesignsprints/

13. Gallo, A. *(2017, November 27). A refresher on A/B testing.* Harvard Business Review. Retrieved March 6, 2023, from https://hbr.org/2017/06/a-refresher-on-ab-testing

14. *Usertesting human insight platform: improve customer experience (CX).* UserTesting. Retrieved March 7, 2023, from https://www.usertesting.com/

15. *User Research & Usability Testing Platform.* UsabilityHub. *(n.d.).* Retrieved March 7, 2023, from https://usabilityhub.com/

16. *The user research recruiting platform for teams.* User Interviews. *(n.d.).* Retrieved March 7, 2023, from https://www.userinterviews.com/

17. Maze. *(2023, February 24). The continuous product discovery platform.* Maze. Retrieved March 7, 2023, from https://maze.co/

## Chapter 10: Advantages of Using Two Hour Design Sprints

1. *Starbucks delivers: Starbucks Coffee Company.* Starbucks Delivers: Starbucks Coffee Company. *(n.d.).* Retrieved March 7, 2023, from https://www.starbucks.com/ways-to-order/delivery

2. *2 hour design sprints: Figma community.* Figma. *(n.d.).* Retrieved March 7, 2023, from https://www.figma.com/community/file/1199463622528181509

3. Webex. *(2023, February 24). Video conferencing, cloud*

*calling & screen sharing: Webex by Cisco.* Webex. Retrieved March 7, 2023, from https://www.webex.com/

4. *Attendee attention tracking – zoom support. (n.d.).* Retrieved March 7, 2023, from https://support.zoom.us/ hc/en-us/articles/115000538083-Attendee-Attention-Tracking

5. *View and export activity logs – figma help center. (n.d.).* Retrieved March 7, 2023, from https://help.figma.com/ hc/en-us/articles/360040449533-View-and-export-activity-logs

6. Balsamiq Cloud. *(n.d.).* Retrieved March 7, 2023, from https://balsamiq.cloud/

7. *Intelligent diagramming.* Lucidchart. *(n.d.).* Retrieved March 7, 2023, from https://www.lucidchart.com/ pages/

8. *CANVA | Free design tool: Presentations, video, social media. (n.d.).* Retrieved March 7, 2023, from https:// www.canva.com/

## Chapter 11: Additional Prep for a Successful Two Hour Design Sprint

1. Cain, T. *(2023, March 6). 2 hour design sprints.* Udemy. Retrieved March 7, 2023, from https://www. udemy.com/course/2hourdesignsprints/?referralCode=3 D0350BD6C05D09D290F

2. *One platform to connect.* Zoom. *(n.d.).* Retrieved March 7, 2023, from https://zoom.us/

3. *Microsoft teams.* Video Conferencing, Meetings, Calling. *(n.d.).* Retrieved March 7, 2023, from https:// www.microsoft.com/en-us/microsoft-teams/group-

chat-software

4.  Google. *(n.d.).* Google meet: Online video meetings and calls | google workspace. Retrieved March 7, 2023, from https://meet.google.com/

## Chapter 12: Conduct Your Two Hour Design Sprint

1.  *2 hour design sprints: Figma community.* Figma. *(n.d.).* Retrieved March 7, 2023, from https://www.figma.com/community/file/1199463622528181509

2.  Cain, T. *(2023, March 6). 2 hour design sprints.* Udemy. Retrieved March 7, 2023, from https://www.udemy.com/course/2hourdesignsprints/?referralCode=3D0350BD6C05D09D290F

## Chapter 13 : After the Two Hour Design Sprint

1.  Knapp, J., Kowitz, B., & Zeratsky, J. *(n.d.).* Sprint: *How to solve big problems and test new ideas in just five days.* Sprint. Retrieved March 5, 2023, from https://www.thesprintbook.com/book

2.  McCarthy, B., & Appel, M. *(n.d.). Aligned.* O'Reilly Online Learning. Retrieved March 6, 2023, from https://www.oreilly.com/library/view/aligned/9781098134419/

3.  *Backlog grooming.* What is Backlog Grooming? | Definition and Overview. *(2021, September 9).* Retrieved March 7, 2023, from https://www.productplan.com/glossary/backlog-grooming/

4.  *Welcome to DevStride.* DevStride. *(n.d.).* Retrieved March 7, 2023, from https://www.devstride.com/

5.   Unlock your team's best work with Jira Software. *(n.d.)*. Retrieved March 7, 2023, from https://jira.atlassian.com/

6.   *Trello brings all your tasks, teammates, and tools together.* Trello. *(n.d.)*. Retrieved March 7, 2023, from https://trello.com/

## On-demand Training for Two Hour Design Sprints

1.   Cain, T. *(2023, March 6). 2 hour design sprints.* Udemy. Retrieved March 7, 2023, from https://www.udemy.com/course/2hourdesignsprints/?referralCode=3D0350BD6C05D09D290F

2.   *2 hour design sprints: Figma community.* Figma. *(n.d.)*. Retrieved March 7, 2023, from https://www.figma.com/community/file/1199463622528181509

# *ACKNOWLEDGEMENTS*

Thanks to IDEO, Stanford's d.school the Hasso Plattner Institute of Design and Jake Knapp, John Zeratsky, Braden Kowitz and Google Ventures for being thought leaders in the industry and the inspiration behind this hybrid method. Thanks to all those in the product, user experience and design community, entrepreneurs and organizations who share the same passion for creating the best experiences for users and accelerating the development and timelines of new features.

Thank you to Rockhurst University, especially Kelly Byrnes, Craig Sasse, Charlotte Shelton, Tony Tocco, Linda Endecott, Joni Lindquist, and Grace Irwin for the motivation and support for this book as part of my Executive MBA journey, and to my entire 2023 cohort for providing support, feedback and friendship along the way. Thank you to Carnegie Mellon University's Integrated Innovation Institute, especially Susanna Slotnikov and Carly Ochs for inspiring me during my pursuit of my Master of Integrated Innovation for Products and Services.

Thank you to Bill Staikos for writing the foreword and inspiring me as a UX practitioner, Melissa Kearney for editing my many late night of rewrites, Kerry Ellis for cover and interior and her creative energy and focus, Heidi Cossins for creative consulting, and John Kille for writing the interlude and being my partner on running workshops and as a thought leader. Thank you to Ruben Betancourt, Diana Stepner and Brian Cox for sharing your experiences after implementing the two hour design sprint process. To my TreviPay teammates Alesandro Meléndez, Courtney Buchmann, Collin Williamson, Emily Farabi and Angela Skalberg-Mander, thank you for your support in testing out and running this method the past few years, and to my boss Dan Zimmerman and TreviPay for supporting me on this journey and trusting in me to create the best methods and training for our teams to support TreviPay's mission of helping businesses grow, and share best practices with other organizations across the globe.